TEACHER'S PET PUBLICATIONS

PUZZLE PACK
for
Romeo And Juliet

based on the play by
William Shakespeare

Written by
William T. Collins

© 2005 Teacher's Pet Publications
All Rights Reserved

The materials in this packet are copyrighted
by Teacher's Pet Publications, Inc.

These pages may be duplicated by the purchaser
for use in the purchaser's own classroom.

Copying any of these materials and distributing them
for any other purpose is a violation of the copyright laws.

© 2005 Teacher's Pet Publications, Inc.
www.tpet.com

INTRODUCTION
If you already own the LitPlan for this title, this Puzzle Pack will refresh your Unit Resource Materials and Vocabulary Resource Materials sections plus give you additional materials you can substitute into the tests. If you do not already have a complete LitPlan, these pages will give you some supplemental materials to use with your own plan. There are two main groups of materials: one set for unit words (such as characters' names, symbols, places, etc.) and one set for vocabulary words associated with the book.

WORD LIST
There is a word list for both the unit words and the vocabulary words. These lists show you which words are being used in the materials and the clues or definitions being used for those words. You may want to give students a word list with clues/definitions to help them, or you may want students to only have a word list (without clues/definitions) if you want them to work a little harder. Both are available for duplication. The word lists can also be your "calling key" for the bingo games.

FILL IN THE BLANK AND MATCHING
There are 4 each of the fill in the blank and matching worksheets for both the unit and vocabulary words. These pages can be used either as extra worksheets for students or as objective parts of a unit test. They can be done individually if students need extra help or as a whole class activity to review the material covered.

MAGIC SQUARES
The magic squares not only reinforce the material covered but also work on reasoning and math skills. Many teachers have told us that their students really enjoy doing these!

WORD SEARCH PUZZLES
The word search words go in all directions, as indicated on your answer keys. Two of the word search puzzles have the clues listed rather than the words. This makes the puzzle a little more difficult, but it reinforces the material better. Two word search puzzles have words only for students who find the clue puzzles too difficult.

CROSSWORD PUZZLES
Both unit and vocabulary word sections have 4 crossword puzzles.

BINGO CARDS
There are 32 individual bingo cards for the unit words and 32 individual bingo cards for the vocabulary words. You can use your word list as a "call list," calling the words at random and marking them off of your list as you go, or you could use the flash cards by cutting them apart and drawing the words at random from a hat (or box or whatever). To make a better review, you might ask for the definition and spelling of each word as you call it out–or you could call out the definitions and have students tell you the words they need to look for on the puzzle.

JUGGLE LETTERS
The vocabulary juggle letter game is intended to help students learn the spellings of the words. One sheet has the definitions listed on it as an extra help for students who need it or to reinforce the definitions if you choose to do so.

FLASH CARDS
We've included a set of vocabulary flash cards you can duplicate, cut, and fold for your students. Some teachers make a few sets for general use by the class; others make a set for each student. Some teachers duplicate them for each student and have the students cut & fold their own. You can cut out just the words and put them in a hat, have each student pick out one word and write the definition and a sentence for that word. Students then swap words and papers, with the next student adding a sentence of his own under the last one. You can have students swap as many times as you like. Each time the student will read the sentences written prior to his own and then add a sentence. You can cut out the words and definitions separately and play "I Have; Who Has?" Each student in the room draws a word and definition. The first student says, "I have (the name of the word). Who has the definition?" The student with the definition reads it then says, "I have (the name of the vocabulary word she has). Who has the definition?" The round continues until all words and definitions have been given.

Romeo & Juliet Word List

No.	Word	Clue/Definition
1.	ACT	Play division
2.	BALTHASAR	Servant to Romeo
3.	BENVOLIO	He explains the circumstances of Tybalt's death.
4.	CAPULET	He gives a feast to introduce Juliet to bachelors.
5.	CRUTCH	A _____, a _____! Why call you for your sword?
6.	DAGGER	Juliet kills herself with Romeo's
7.	DEATH	_____ is my son-in-law, _____ is my heir.
8.	FATE	Predestined future
9.	FOE	My life is my __'s debt.
10.	GRIEVING	Lady Montague dies ___ for her son, Romeo.
11.	JULIET	Both Paris and Romeo want to marry her.
12.	LADY	She wants the Prince to execute Romeo: ___ Capulet
13.	LAURENCE	He agrees to marry Romeo & Juliet: Friar ___
14.	MERCUTIO	He is slain by Tybalt.
15.	MONTAGUE	Romeo's father
16.	ORCHARD	Romeo climbs over the wall surrounding Capulet's _____.
17.	PLAGUE	A ____ o'both your houses.
18.	POISON	Romeo drinks it and dies.
19.	PRINCE	Sends Romeo into exile
20.	ROMEO	He kills himself when he thinks Juliet is dead.
21.	ROSALINE	She refused Romeo's love and caused his depression.
22.	ROSE	That which we call a _____ By any other name would smell as sweet.
23.	SAMSON	Servant of the Capulets
24.	SCENE	Act division
25.	SHAKESPEARE	Author William
26.	SORROW	Parting is such sweet _____.
27.	TOMB	Me thinks I see thee .... as one dead in the bottom of a _____.
28.	TYBALT	Romeo kills him to avenge his friend's death.
29.	UNDONE	We are _____, lady, we are _____.
30.	VERONA	Paris is a nobleman from this place.
31.	WINDOW	What light through yonder _____ breaks?

Romeo & Juliet Fill In The Blanks 1

_____

_____

_____

_____

_____

_____

_____

_____

_____

_____

_____

_____

_____

_____

_____

_____

_____

_____

_____

_____

1. Lady Montague dies ___ for her son, Romeo.
2. Servant of the Capulets
3. He gives a feast to introduce Juliet to bachelors.
4. Act division
5. My life is my __'s debt.
6. Juliet kills herself with Romeo's
7. He explains the circumstances of Tybalt's death.
8. Romeo drinks it and dies.
9. Paris is a nobleman from this place.
10. She wants the Prince to execute Romeo: ___ Capulet
11. Me thinks I see thee .... as one dead in the bottom of a _____.
12. Parting is such sweet _____.
13. She refused Romeo's love and caused his depression.
14. Predestined future
15. Servant to Romeo
16. We are _____, lady, we are _____.
17. Author William
18. A _____, a _____! Why call you for your sword?
19. Both Paris and Romeo want to marry her.
20. _____ is my son-in-law, _____ is my heir.

Romeo & Juliet Fill In The Blanks 1 Answer Key

GRIEVING	1. Lady Montague dies ___ for her son, Romeo.
SAMSON	2. Servant of the Capulets
CAPULET	3. He gives a feast to introduce Juliet to bachelors.
SCENE	4. Act division
FOE	5. My life is my __'s debt.
DAGGER	6. Juliet kills herself with Romeo's
BENVOLIO	7. He explains the circumstances of Tybalt's death.
POISON	8. Romeo drinks it and dies.
VERONA	9. Paris is a nobleman from this place.
LADY	10. She wants the Prince to execute Romeo: ___ Capulet
TOMB	11. Me thinks I see thee .... as one dead in the bottom of a _____.
SORROW	12. Parting is such sweet _____.
ROSALINE	13. She refused Romeo's love and caused his depression.
FATE	14. Predestined future
BALTHASAR	15. Servant to Romeo
UNDONE	16. We are _____, lady, we are _____.
SHAKESPEARE	17. Author William
CRUTCH	18. A _____, a _____! Why call you for your sword?
JULIET	19. Both Paris and Romeo want to marry her.
DEATH	20. _____ is my son-in-law, _____ is my heir.

Romeo & Juliet Fill In The Blanks 2

_____
_____
_____
_____
_____
_____
_____
_____
_____
_____
_____
_____
_____
_____
_____
_____
_____
_____
_____
_____

1. Play division
2. Romeo kills him to avenge his friend's death.
3. A _____, a _____! Why call you for your sword?
4. Servant to Romeo
5. She refused Romeo's love and caused his depression.
6. We are _____, lady, we are _____.
7. Both Paris and Romeo want to marry her.
8. Romeo climbs over the wall surrounding Capulet's _____.
9. Paris is a nobleman from this place.
10. Romeo drinks it and dies.
11. Lady Montague dies ___ for her son, Romeo.
12. He explains the circumstances of Tybalt's death.
13. He kills himself when he thinks Juliet is dead.
14. Romeo's father
15. Act division
16. Servant of the Capulets
17. _____ is my son-in-law, _____ is my heir.
18. Me thinks I see thee .... as one dead in the bottom of a _____.
19. Sends Romeo into exile
20. He gives a feast to introduce Juliet to bachelors.

Romeo & Juliet Fill In The Blanks 2 Answer Key

ACT	1. Play division
TYBALT	2. Romeo kills him to avenge his friend's death.
CRUTCH	3. A _____, a _____! Why call you for your sword?
BALTHASAR	4. Servant to Romeo
ROSALINE	5. She refused Romeo's love and caused his depression.
UNDONE	6. We are _____, lady, we are _____.
JULIET	7. Both Paris and Romeo want to marry her.
ORCHARD	8. Romeo climbs over the wall surrounding Capulet's _____.
VERONA	9. Paris is a nobleman from this place.
POISON	10. Romeo drinks it and dies.
GRIEVING	11. Lady Montague dies ___ for her son, Romeo.
BENVOLIO	12. He explains the circumstances of Tybalt's death.
ROMEO	13. He kills himself when he thinks Juliet is dead.
MONTAGUE	14. Romeo's father
SCENE	15. Act division
SAMSON	16. Servant of the Capulets
DEATH	17. _____ is my son-in-law, _____ is my heir.
TOMB	18. Me thinks I see thee .... as one dead in the bottom of a _____.
PRINCE	19. Sends Romeo into exile
CAPULET	20. He gives a feast to introduce Juliet to bachelors.

Romeo & Juliet Fill In The Blanks 3

_____
_____
_____
_____
_____
_____
_____
_____
_____
_____
_____
_____
_____
_____
_____
_____
_____
_____
_____
_____

1. Sends Romeo into exile
2. He kills himself when he thinks Juliet is dead.
3. She wants the Prince to execute Romeo: ___ Capulet
4. _____ is my son-in-law, _____ is my heir.
5. She refused Romeo's love and caused his depression.
6. Parting is such sweet _____.
7. Both Paris and Romeo want to marry her.
8. Paris is a nobleman from this place.
9. Play division
10. Romeo climbs over the wall surrounding Capulet's _____.
11. Act division
12. Predestined future
13. Lady Montague dies ___ for her son, Romeo.
14. Me thinks I see thee .... as one dead in the bottom of a _____.
15. He is slain by Tybalt.
16. Romeo drinks it and dies.
17. My life is my __'s debt.
18. We are _____, lady, we are _____.
19. Servant of the Capulets
20. Juliet kills herself with Romeo's

Romeo & Juliet Fill In The Blanks 3 Answer Key

Answer	Clue
PRINCE	1. Sends Romeo into exile
ROMEO	2. He kills himself when he thinks Juliet is dead.
LADY	3. She wants the Prince to execute Romeo: ___ Capulet
DEATH	4. _____ is my son-in-law, _____ is my heir.
ROSALINE	5. She refused Romeo's love and caused his depression.
SORROW	6. Parting is such sweet _____.
JULIET	7. Both Paris and Romeo want to marry her.
VERONA	8. Paris is a nobleman from this place.
ACT	9. Play division
ORCHARD	10. Romeo climbs over the wall surrounding Capulet's _____.
SCENE	11. Act division
FATE	12. Predestined future
GRIEVING	13. Lady Montague dies ___ for her son, Romeo.
TOMB	14. Me thinks I see thee .... as one dead in the bottom of a _____.
MERCUTIO	15. He is slain by Tybalt.
POISON	16. Romeo drinks it and dies.
FOE	17. My life is my __'s debt.
UNDONE	18. We are _____, lady, we are _____.
SAMSON	19. Servant of the Capulets
DAGGER	20. Juliet kills herself with Romeo's

Romeo & Juliet Fill In The Blanks 4

_____
_____
_____
_____
_____
_____
_____
_____
_____
_____
_____
_____
_____
_____
_____
_____
_____
_____
_____
_____

1. He kills himself when he thinks Juliet is dead.
2. Me thinks I see thee .... as one dead in the bottom of a _____.
3. He explains the circumstances of Tybalt's death.
4. Predestined future
5. Author William
6. She refused Romeo's love and caused his depression.
7. _____ is my son-in-law, _____ is my heir.
8. A _____, a _____! Why call you for your sword?
9. She wants the Prince to execute Romeo: ___ Capulet
10. Romeo drinks it and dies.
11. Romeo climbs over the wall surrounding Capulet's _____.
12. Sends Romeo into exile
13. Servant to Romeo
14. Play division
15. That which we call a _____ By any other name would smell as sweet.
16. What light through yonder _____ breaks?
17. He agrees to marry Romeo & Juliet: Friar ___
18. Romeo kills him to avenge his friend's death.
19. He gives a feast to introduce Juliet to bachelors.
20. My life is my __'s debt.

Romeo & Juliet Fill In The Blanks 4 Answer Key

ROMEO	1. He kills himself when he thinks Juliet is dead.
TOMB	2. Me thinks I see thee .... as one dead in the bottom of a _____.
BENVOLIO	3. He explains the circumstances of Tybalt's death.
FATE	4. Predestined future
SHAKESPEARE	5. Author William
ROSALINE	6. She refused Romeo's love and caused his depression.
DEATH	7. _____ is my son-in-law, _____ is my heir.
CRUTCH	8. A _____, a _____! Why call you for your sword?
LADY	9. She wants the Prince to execute Romeo: ___ Capulet
POISON	10. Romeo drinks it and dies.
ORCHARD	11. Romeo climbs over the wall surrounding Capulet's _____.
PRINCE	12. Sends Romeo into exile
BALTHASAR	13. Servant to Romeo
ACT	14. Play division
ROSE	15. That which we call a _____ By any other name would smell as sweet.
WINDOW	16. What light through yonder _____ breaks?
LAURENCE	17. He agrees to marry Romeo & Juliet: Friar ___
TYBALT	18. Romeo kills him to avenge his friend's death.
CAPULET	19. He gives a feast to introduce Juliet to bachelors.
FOE	20. My life is my __'s debt.

Romeo & Juliet Matching 1

___ 1. WINDOW   A. Romeo kills him to avenge his friend's death.
___ 2. LAURENCE   B. Lady Montague dies ___ for her son, Romeo.
___ 3. CRUTCH   C. Act division
___ 4. SORROW   D. What light through yonder _____ breaks?
___ 5. FOE   E. Romeo drinks it and dies.
___ 6. ROSE   F. Romeo's father
___ 7. POISON   G. A _____, a _____! Why call you for your sword?
___ 8. BENVOLIO   H. Juliet kills herself with Romeo's
___ 9. MERCUTIO   I. He gives a feast to introduce Juliet to bachelors.
___10. DAGGER   J. We are _____, lady, we are _____.
___11. DEATH   K. _____ is my son-in-law, _____ is my heir.
___12. PLAGUE   L. Play division
___13. TOMB   M. A ____ o'both your houses.
___14. CAPULET   N. He is slain by Tybalt.
___15. LADY   O. She wants the Prince to execute Romeo: ___ Capulet
___16. GRIEVING   P. Romeo climbs over the wall surrounding Capulet's _____.
___17. BALTHASAR   Q. Parting is such sweet _____.
___18. ROMEO   R. He kills himself when he thinks Juliet is dead.
___19. SCENE   S. Both Paris and Romeo want to marry her.
___20. TYBALT   T. Me thinks I see thee .... as one dead in the bottom of a _____.
___21. ORCHARD   U. He agrees to marry Romeo & Juliet: Friar ___
___22. UNDONE   V. He explains the circumstances of Tybalt's death.
___23. JULIET   W. Servant to Romeo
___24. MONTAGUE   X. That which we call a _____ By any other name would smell as sweet.
___25. ACT   Y. My life is my __'s debt.

13
Copyrighted

Romeo & Juliet Matching 1 Answer Key

D - 1. WINDOW	A. Romeo kills him to avenge his friend's death.
U - 2. LAURENCE	B. Lady Montague dies ___ for her son, Romeo.
G - 3. CRUTCH	C. Act division
Q - 4. SORROW	D. What light through yonder _____ breaks?
Y - 5. FOE	E. Romeo drinks it and dies.
X - 6. ROSE	F. Romeo's father
E - 7. POISON	G. A _____, a _____! Why call you for your sword?
V - 8. BENVOLIO	H. Juliet kills herself with Romeo's
N - 9. MERCUTIO	I. He gives a feast to introduce Juliet to bachelors.
H - 10. DAGGER	J. We are _____, lady, we are _____.
K - 11. DEATH	K. _____ is my son-in-law, _____ is my heir.
M - 12. PLAGUE	L. Play division
T - 13. TOMB	M. A ____ o'both your houses.
I - 14. CAPULET	N. He is slain by Tybalt.
O - 15. LADY	O. She wants the Prince to execute Romeo: ___ Capulet
B - 16. GRIEVING	P. Romeo climbs over the wall surrounding Capulet's _____.
W - 17. BALTHASAR	Q. Parting is such sweet _____.
R - 18. ROMEO	R. He kills himself when he thinks Juliet is dead.
C - 19. SCENE	S. Both Paris and Romeo want to marry her.
A - 20. TYBALT	T. Me thinks I see thee .... as one dead in the bottom of a _____.
P - 21. ORCHARD	U. He agrees to marry Romeo & Juliet: Friar ___
J - 22. UNDONE	V. He explains the circumstances of Tybalt's death.
S - 23. JULIET	W. Servant to Romeo
F - 24. MONTAGUE	X. That which we call a _____ By any other name would smell as sweet.
L - 25. ACT	Y. My life is my __'s debt.

Romeo & Juliet Matching 2

___ 1. ROSALINE   A. What light through yonder _____ breaks?
___ 2. ROSE   B. A _____, a _____! Why call you for your sword?
___ 3. POISON   C. She wants the Prince to execute Romeo: ___ Capulet
___ 4. ACT   D. That which we call a _____ By any other name would smell as sweet.
___ 5. SORROW   E. He agrees to marry Romeo & Juliet: Friar ___
___ 6. FOE   F. Predestined future
___ 7. CAPULET   G. Sends Romeo into exile
___ 8. SAMSON   H. We are _____, lady, we are _____.
___ 9. LADY   I. Lady Montague dies ___ for her son, Romeo.
___10. SCENE   J. My life is my __'s debt.
___11. CRUTCH   K. Romeo climbs over the wall surrounding Capulet's _____.
___12. BALTHASAR   L. Me thinks I see thee .... as one dead in the bottom of a _____.
___13. ORCHARD   M. Servant to Romeo
___14. GRIEVING   N. Act division
___15. WINDOW   O. Romeo drinks it and dies.
___16. TYBALT   P. Servant of the Capulets
___17. UNDONE   Q. She refused Romeo's love and caused his depression.
___18. JULIET   R. Paris is a nobleman from this place.
___19. FATE   S. Romeo kills him to avenge his friend's death.
___20. TOMB   T. Parting is such sweet _____.
___21. LAURENCE   U. He explains the circumstances of Tybalt's death.
___22. VERONA   V. Romeo's father
___23. BENVOLIO   W. He gives a feast to introduce Juliet to bachelors.
___24. MONTAGUE   X. Both Paris and Romeo want to marry her.
___25. PRINCE   Y. Play division

Romeo & Juliet Matching 2 Answer Key

Q - 1. ROSALINE   A. What light through yonder _____ breaks?
D - 2. ROSE   B. A _____, a _____! Why call you for your sword?
O - 3. POISON   C. She wants the Prince to execute Romeo: ___ Capulet
Y - 4. ACT   D. That which we call a _____ By any other name would smell as sweet.
T - 5. SORROW   E. He agrees to marry Romeo & Juliet: Friar ___
J - 6. FOE   F. Predestined future
W - 7. CAPULET   G. Sends Romeo into exile
P - 8. SAMSON   H. We are _____, lady, we are _____.
C - 9. LADY   I. Lady Montague dies ___ for her son, Romeo.
N - 10. SCENE   J. My life is my __'s debt.
B - 11. CRUTCH   K. Romeo climbs over the wall surrounding Capulet's _____.
M - 12. BALTHASAR   L. Me thinks I see thee .... as one dead in the bottom of a _____.
K - 13. ORCHARD   M. Servant to Romeo
I - 14. GRIEVING   N. Act division
A - 15. WINDOW   O. Romeo drinks it and dies.
S - 16. TYBALT   P. Servant of the Capulets
H - 17. UNDONE   Q. She refused Romeo's love and caused his depression.
X - 18. JULIET   R. Paris is a nobleman from this place.
F - 19. FATE   S. Romeo kills him to avenge his friend's death.
L - 20. TOMB   T. Parting is such sweet _____.
E - 21. LAURENCE   U. He explains the circumstances of Tybalt's death.
R - 22. VERONA   V. Romeo's father
U - 23. BENVOLIO   W. He gives a feast to introduce Juliet to bachelors.
V - 24. MONTAGUE   X. Both Paris and Romeo want to marry her.
G - 25. PRINCE   Y. Play division

Romeo & Juliet Matching 3

___ 1. UNDONE	A. He kills himself when he thinks Juliet is dead.
___ 2. TYBALT	B. Romeo's father
___ 3. VERONA	C. She refused Romeo's love and caused his depression.
___ 4. SAMSON	D. Servant of the Capulets
___ 5. CAPULET	E. Romeo climbs over the wall surrounding Capulet's _____.
___ 6. TOMB	F. A ____ o'both your houses.
___ 7. JULIET	G. What light through yonder _____ breaks?
___ 8. PLAGUE	H. Paris is a nobleman from this place.
___ 9. BALTHASAR	I. Play division
___10. DEATH	J. Juliet kills herself with Romeo's
___11. MERCUTIO	K. Me thinks I see thee .... as one dead in the bottom of a _____.
___12. PRINCE	L. Both Paris and Romeo want to marry her.
___13. WINDOW	M. My life is my __'s debt.
___14. ROSALINE	N. He agrees to marry Romeo & Juliet: Friar ___
___15. BENVOLIO	O. Romeo kills him to avenge his friend's death.
___16. ROMEO	P. That which we call a _____ By any other name would smell as sweet.
___17. ROSE	Q. Predestined future
___18. FOE	R. He is slain by Tybalt.
___19. ACT	S. He explains the circumstances of Tybalt's death.
___20. MONTAGUE	T. Sends Romeo into exile
___21. LADY	U. _____ is my son-in-law, _____ is my heir.
___22. FATE	V. Servant to Romeo
___23. ORCHARD	W. We are _____, lady, we are _____.
___24. DAGGER	X. She wants the Prince to execute Romeo: ___ Capulet
___25. LAURENCE	Y. He gives a feast to introduce Juliet to bachelors.

Romeo & Juliet Matching 3 Answer Key

W - 1. UNDONE	A.	He kills himself when he thinks Juliet is dead.
O - 2. TYBALT	B.	Romeo's father
H - 3. VERONA	C.	She refused Romeo's love and caused his depression.
D - 4. SAMSON	D.	Servant of the Capulets
Y - 5. CAPULET	E.	Romeo climbs over the wall surrounding Capulet's _____.
K - 6. TOMB	F.	A ____ o'both your houses.
L - 7. JULIET	G.	What light through yonder _____ breaks?
F - 8. PLAGUE	H.	Paris is a nobleman from this place.
V - 9. BALTHASAR	I.	Play division
U -10. DEATH	J.	Juliet kills herself with Romeo's
R -11. MERCUTIO	K.	Me thinks I see thee .... as one dead in the bottom of a _____.
T -12. PRINCE	L.	Both Paris and Romeo want to marry her.
G -13. WINDOW	M.	My life is my __'s debt.
C -14. ROSALINE	N.	He agrees to marry Romeo & Juliet: Friar ___
S -15. BENVOLIO	O.	Romeo kills him to avenge his friend's death.
A -16. ROMEO	P.	That which we call a _____ By any other name would smell as sweet.
P -17. ROSE	Q.	Predestined future
M -18. FOE	R.	He is slain by Tybalt.
I - 19. ACT	S.	He explains the circumstances of Tybalt's death.
B -20. MONTAGUE	T.	Sends Romeo into exile
X -21. LADY	U.	_____ is my son-in-law, _____ is my heir.
Q -22. FATE	V.	Servant to Romeo
E -23. ORCHARD	W.	We are _____, lady, we are _____.
J -24. DAGGER	X.	She wants the Prince to execute Romeo: ___ Capulet
N -25. LAURENCE	Y.	He gives a feast to introduce Juliet to bachelors.

Romeo & Juliet Matching 4

___ 1. BALTHASAR   A. Romeo climbs over the wall surrounding Capulet's _____.
___ 2. MONTAGUE   B. He agrees to marry Romeo & Juliet: Friar ___
___ 3. FOE   C. Lady Montague dies ___ for her son, Romeo.
___ 4. SCENE   D. A ____ o'both your houses.
___ 5. SHAKESPEARE   E. Servant to Romeo
___ 6. BENVOLIO   F. Parting is such sweet _____.
___ 7. LAURENCE   G. We are _____, lady, we are _____.
___ 8. CRUTCH   H. She wants the Prince to execute Romeo: ___ Capulet
___ 9. ROSE   I. Author William
___ 10. WINDOW   J. Sends Romeo into exile
___ 11. POISON   K. Play division
___ 12. DAGGER   L. Act division
___ 13. LADY   M. She refused Romeo's love and caused his depression.
___ 14. ACT   N. He gives a feast to introduce Juliet to bachelors.
___ 15. UNDONE   O. Both Paris and Romeo want to marry her.
___ 16. SORROW   P. Romeo's father
___ 17. ORCHARD   Q. Juliet kills herself with Romeo's
___ 18. FATE   R. What light through yonder _____ breaks?
___ 19. JULIET   S. My life is my __'s debt.
___ 20. CAPULET   T. Servant of the Capulets
___ 21. GRIEVING   U. That which we call a _____ By any other name would smell as sweet.
___ 22. ROSALINE   V. Predestined future
___ 23. PRINCE   W. A _____, a _____! Why call you for your sword?
___ 24. SAMSON   X. Romeo drinks it and dies.
___ 25. PLAGUE   Y. He explains the circumstances of Tybalt's death.

Romeo & Juliet Matching 4 Answer Key

E - 1. BALTHASAR	A.	Romeo climbs over the wall surrounding Capulet's _____.
P - 2. MONTAGUE	B.	He agrees to marry Romeo & Juliet: Friar ___
S - 3. FOE	C.	Lady Montague dies ___ for her son, Romeo.
L - 4. SCENE	D.	A ____ o'both your houses.
I - 5. SHAKESPEARE	E.	Servant to Romeo
Y - 6. BENVOLIO	F.	Parting is such sweet _____.
B - 7. LAURENCE	G.	We are _____, lady, we are _____.
W - 8. CRUTCH	H.	She wants the Prince to execute Romeo: ___ Capulet
U - 9. ROSE	I.	Author William
R - 10. WINDOW	J.	Sends Romeo into exile
X - 11. POISON	K.	Play division
Q - 12. DAGGER	L.	Act division
H - 13. LADY	M.	She refused Romeo's love and caused his depression.
K - 14. ACT	N.	He gives a feast to introduce Juliet to bachelors.
G - 15. UNDONE	O.	Both Paris and Romeo want to marry her.
F - 16. SORROW	P.	Romeo's father
A - 17. ORCHARD	Q.	Juliet kills herself with Romeo's
V - 18. FATE	R.	What light through yonder _____ breaks?
O - 19. JULIET	S.	My life is my __'s debt.
N - 20. CAPULET	T.	Servant of the Capulets
C - 21. GRIEVING	U.	That which we call a _____ By any other name would smell as sweet.
M - 22. ROSALINE	V.	Predestined future
J - 23. PRINCE	W.	A _____, a _____! Why call you for your sword?
T - 24. SAMSON	X.	Romeo drinks it and dies.
D - 25. PLAGUE	Y.	He explains the circumstances of Tybalt's death.

Romeo & Juliet Magic Squares 1

Match the definition with the vocabulary word. Put your answers in the magic squares below. When your answers are correct, all columns and rows will add to the same number.

A. DEATH
B. WINDOW
C. SORROW
D. CRUTCH
E. CAPULET
F. TYBALT
G. UNDONE
H. FOE
I. MONTAGUE
J. PLAGUE
K. MERCUTIO
L. FATE
M. LAURENCE
N. ROMEO
O. BALTHASAR
P. ORCHARD

1. Servant to Romeo
2. A _____, a _____! Why call you for your sword?
3. A ____ o'both your houses.
4. He gives a feast to introduce Juliet to bachelors.
5. Romeo's father
6. Romeo kills him to avenge his friend's death.
7. Romeo climbs over the wall surrounding Capulet's _____.
8. Parting is such sweet _____.
9. My life is my __'s debt.
10. He is slain by Tybalt.
11. _____ is my son-in-law, _____ is my heir.
12. He kills himself when he thinks Juliet is dead.
13. What light through yonder _____ breaks?
14. He agrees to marry Romeo & Juliet: Friar ___
15. We are _____, lady, we are _____.
16. Predestined future

A=	B=	C=	D=
E=	F=	G=	H=
I=	J=	K=	L=
M=	N=	O=	P=

Romeo & Juliet Magic Squares 1 Answer Key

Match the definition with the vocabulary word. Put your answers in the magic squares below. When your answers are correct, all columns and rows will add to the same number.

A. DEATH
B. WINDOW
C. SORROW
D. CRUTCH
E. CAPULET
F. TYBALT
G. UNDONE
H. FOE
I. MONTAGUE
J. PLAGUE
K. MERCUTIO
L. FATE
M. LAURENCE
N. ROMEO
O. BALTHASAR
P. ORCHARD

1. Servant to Romeo
2. A _____, a _____! Why call you for your sword?
3. A ____ o'both your houses.
4. He gives a feast to introduce Juliet to bachelors.
5. Romeo's father
6. Romeo kills him to avenge his friend's death.
7. Romeo climbs over the wall surrounding Capulet's _____.
8. Parting is such sweet _____.
9. My life is my __'s debt.
10. He is slain by Tybalt.
11. _____ is my son-in-law, _____ is my heir.
12. He kills himself when he thinks Juliet is dead.
13. What light through yonder _____ breaks?
14. He agrees to marry Romeo & Juliet: Friar ___
15. We are _____, lady, we are _____.
16. Predestined future

A=11	B=13	C=8	D=2
E=4	F=6	G=15	H=9
I=5	J=3	K=10	L=16
M=14	N=12	O=1	P=7

22
Copyrighted

Romeo & Juliet Magic Squares 2

Match the definition with the vocabulary word. Put your answers in the magic squares below. When your answers are correct, all columns and rows will add to the same number.

A. MERCUTIO
B. FATE
C. ORCHARD
D. VERONA
E. PLAGUE
F. SHAKESPEARE
G. DAGGER
H. SORROW
I. SAMSON
J. ROMEO
K. CAPULET
L. POISON
M. SCENE
N. UNDONE
O. BALTHASAR
P. ACT

1. He is slain by Tybalt.
2. We are _____, lady, we are _____.
3. He kills himself when he thinks Juliet is dead.
4. A ____ o'both your houses.
5. Juliet kills herself with Romeo's
6. Romeo drinks it and dies.
7. Play division
8. Romeo climbs over the wall surrounding Capulet's _____.
9. Servant to Romeo
10. Paris is a nobleman from this place.
11. Parting is such sweet _____.
12. He gives a feast to introduce Juliet to bachelors.
13. Servant of the Capulets
14. Author William
15. Predestined future
16. Act division

A=	B=	C=	D=
E=	F=	G=	H=
I=	J=	K=	L=
M=	N=	O=	P=

Romeo & Juliet Magic Squares 2 Answer Key

Match the definition with the vocabulary word. Put your answers in the magic squares below. When your answers are correct, all columns and rows will add to the same number.

A. MERCUTIO
B. FATE
C. ORCHARD
D. VERONA
E. PLAGUE
F. SHAKESPEARE
G. DAGGER
H. SORROW
I. SAMSON
J. ROMEO
K. CAPULET
L. POISON
M. SCENE
N. UNDONE
O. BALTHASAR
P. ACT

1. He is slain by Tybalt.
2. We are _____, lady, we are _____.
3. He kills himself when he thinks Juliet is dead.
4. A ____ o'both your houses.
5. Juliet kills herself with Romeo's
6. Romeo drinks it and dies.
7. Play division
8. Romeo climbs over the wall surrounding Capulet's _____.
9. Servant to Romeo
10. Paris is a nobleman from this place.
11. Parting is such sweet _____.
12. He gives a feast to introduce Juliet to bachelors.
13. Servant of the Capulets
14. Author William
15. Predestined future
16. Act division

A=1	B=15	C=8	D=10
E=4	F=14	G=5	H=11
I=13	J=3	K=12	L=6
M=16	N=2	O=9	P=7

Romeo & Juliet Magic Squares 3

Match the definition with the vocabulary word. Put your answers in the magic squares below. When your answers are correct, all columns and rows will add to the same number.

A. SHAKESPEARE
B. DAGGER
C. UNDONE
D. DEATH
E. LAURENCE
F. JULIET
G. ACT
H. LADY
I. CRUTCH
J. SORROW
K. ROSALINE
L. PLAGUE
M. MERCUTIO
N. ROSE
O. BENVOLIO
P. FATE

1. We are _____, lady, we are _____.
2. Parting is such sweet _____.
3. Both Paris and Romeo want to marry her.
4. He explains the circumstances of Tybalt's death.
5. Predestined future
6. He agrees to marry Romeo & Juliet: Friar ___
7. A _____, a _____! Why call you for your sword?
8. _____ is my son-in-law, _____ is my heir.
9. He is slain by Tybalt.
10. She wants the Prince to execute Romeo: ___ Capulet
11. A ____ o'both your houses.
12. Author William
13. Juliet kills herself with Romeo's
14. She refused Romeo's love and caused his depression.
15. Play division
16. That which we call a _____ By any other name would smell as sweet. sweet.

A=	B=	C=	D=
E=	F=	G=	H=
I=	J=	K=	L=
M=	N=	O=	P=

Romeo & Juliet Magic Squares 3 Answer Key

Match the definition with the vocabulary word. Put your answers in the magic squares below. When your answers are correct, all columns and rows will add to the same number.

A. SHAKESPEARE
B. DAGGER
C. UNDONE
D. DEATH
E. LAURENCE
F. JULIET
G. ACT
H. LADY
I. CRUTCH
J. SORROW
K. ROSALINE
L. PLAGUE
M. MERCUTIO
N. ROSE
O. BENVOLIO
P. FATE

1. We are _____, lady, we are _____.
2. Parting is such sweet _____.
3. Both Paris and Romeo want to marry her.
4. He explains the circumstances of Tybalt's death.
5. Predestined future
6. He agrees to marry Romeo & Juliet: Friar ___
7. A _____, a _____! Why call you for your sword?
8. _____ is my son-in-law, _____ is my heir.
9. He is slain by Tybalt.
10. She wants the Prince to execute Romeo: ___ Capulet
11. A ____ o'both your houses.
12. Author William
13. Juliet kills herself with Romeo's
14. She refused Romeo's love and caused his depression.
15. Play division
16. That which we call a _____ By any other name would smell as sweet. sweet.

A=12	B=13	C=1	D=8
E=6	F=3	G=15	H=10
I=7	J=2	K=14	L=11
M=9	N=16	O=4	P=5

26
Copyrighted

Romeo & Juliet Magic Squares 4

Match the definition with the vocabulary word. Put your answers in the magic squares below. When your answers are correct, all columns and rows will add to the same number.

A. ORCHARD
B. JULIET
C. PRINCE
D. FOE
E. TOMB
F. SAMSON
G. DEATH
H. SORROW
I. SCENE
J. TYBALT
K. CRUTCH
L. MONTAGUE
M. WINDOW
N. GRIEVING
O. POISON
P. ACT

1. Romeo drinks it and dies.
2. Romeo kills him to avenge his friend's death.
3. Parting is such sweet _____.
4. Romeo climbs over the wall surrounding Capulet's _____.
5. My life is my __'s debt.
6. Me thinks I see thee .... as one dead in the bottom of a _____.
7. A _____, a _____! Why call you for your sword?
8. Lady Montague dies ___ for her son, Romeo.
9. Servant of the Capulets
10. Sends Romeo into exile
11. What light through yonder _____ breaks?
12. Romeo's father
13. Act division
14. Play division
15. Both Paris and Romeo want to marry her.
16. _____ is my son-in-law, _____ is my heir.

A=	B=	C=	D=
E=	F=	G=	H=
I=	J=	K=	L=
M=	N=	O=	P=

27
Copyrighted

Romeo & Juliet Magic Squares 4

Match the definition with the vocabulary word. Put your answers in the magic squares below. When your answers are correct, all columns and rows will add to the same number.

A. ORCHARD
B. JULIET
C. PRINCE
D. FOE
E. TOMB
F. SAMSON
G. DEATH
H. SORROW
I. SCENE
J. TYBALT
K. CRUTCH
L. MONTAGUE
M. WINDOW
N. GRIEVING
O. POISON
P. ACT

1. Romeo drinks it and dies.
2. Romeo kills him to avenge his friend's death.
3. Parting is such sweet _____.
4. Romeo climbs over the wall surrounding Capulet's _____.
5. My life is my __'s debt.
6. Me thinks I see thee .... as one dead in the bottom of a _____.
7. A _____, a _____! Why call you for your sword?
8. Lady Montague dies ___ for her son, Romeo.
9. Servant of the Capulets
10. Sends Romeo into exile
11. What light through yonder _____ breaks?
12. Romeo's father
13. Act division
14. Play division
15. Both Paris and Romeo want to marry her.
16. _____ is my son-in-law, _____ is my heir.

A=4	B=15	C=10	D=5
E=6	F=9	G=16	H=3
I=13	J=2	K=7	L=12
M=11	N=8	O=1	P=14

Romeo & Juliet Word Search 1

Words are placed backwards, forward, diagonally, up and down. Clues listed below can help you find the words. Circle the hidden vocabulary words in the maze.

```
H G F L R R T R B A L T H A S A R L B
G P B A R P B G O Q D W I N D O W J W
H K K D C C R R O S E F N J B C F Q P
S N S Y J U L I E T A Y E S O R L P L
W H D D X Q L E N T T L G B E U A K X
P R A C S O L V E C H S I G S T U M S
L C C V V M B I C S E H G N P C R M D
A F T N V T N N S H Z A D V E H E E J
G Z E W L W O G Q M D K M E J X N B Q
U B B A O W G M X F X E E R R O C O Q
E Z B R C P G E B Q V S R O D M E J J
Q Y R X R A U G J F Q P C N X M F Y H
T O Z K R G P S W W H E U A O C N S Z
S Y S L A V M U E B Q A T R T O O N N
D J J T K J C O L X Q R I G S R S D Z
Y Y N T Y H F N N E C E O I D D M P V
W O P T P J G X R B T T O R C H A R D
M G C W R F W N K N Y P K K D Q S D T
```

A ____ o'both your houses. (6)
A _____, a _____! Why call you for your sword? (6)
Act division (5)
Author William (11)
Both Paris and Romeo want to marry her. (6)
He agrees to marry Romeo & Juliet: Friar ___ (8)
He explains the circumstances of Tybalt's death. (8)
He gives a feast to introduce Juliet to bachelors. (7)
He is slain by Tybalt. (8)
He kills himself when he thinks Juliet is dead. (5)
Juliet kills herself with Romeo's (6)
Lady Montague dies ___ for her son, Romeo. (8)
Me thinks I see thee .... as one dead in the bottom of a _____. (4)
My life is my __'s debt. (3)
Paris is a nobleman from this place. (6)

Parting is such sweet _____. (6)
Play division (3)
Predestined future (4)
Romeo climbs over the wall surrounding Capulet's _____. (7)
Romeo drinks it and dies. (6)
Romeo kills him to avenge his friend's death. (6)
Romeo's father (8)
Sends Romeo into exile (6)
Servant of the Capulets (6)
Servant to Romeo (9)
She refused Romeo's love and caused his depression. (8)
She wants the Prince to execute Romeo: ___ Capulet (4)
That which we call a _____ By any other name would smell as sweet. (4)
We are _____, lady, we are _____. (6)
What light through yonder _____ breaks? (6)
_____ is my son-in-law, _____ is my heir. (5)

Romeo & Juliet Word Search 1 Answer Key

Words are placed backwards, forward, diagonally, up and down. Clues listed below can help you find the words. Circle the hidden vocabulary words in the maze.

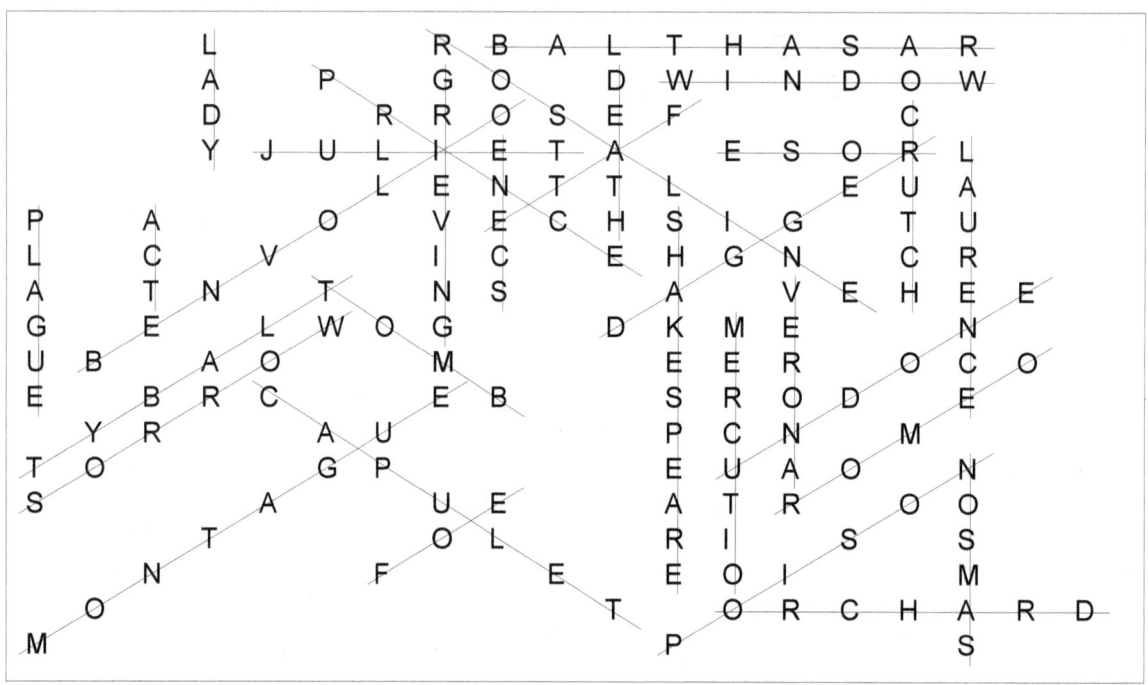

A _____ o'both your houses. (6)
A _____, a _____! Why call you for your sword? (6)
Act division (5)
Author William (11)
Both Paris and Romeo want to marry her. (6)
He agrees to marry Romeo & Juliet: Friar ___ (8)
He explains the circumstances of Tybalt's death. (8)
He gives a feast to introduce Juliet to bachelors. (7)
He is slain by Tybalt. (8)
He kills himself when he thinks Juliet is dead. (5)
Juliet kills herself with Romeo's (6)
Lady Montague dies ___ for her son, Romeo. (8)
Me thinks I see thee .... as one dead in the bottom of a _____. (4)
My life is my __'s debt. (3)
Paris is a nobleman from this place. (6)

Parting is such sweet _____. (6)
Play division (3)
Predestined future (4)
Romeo climbs over the wall surrounding Capulet's _____. (7)
Romeo drinks it and dies. (6)
Romeo kills him to avenge his friend's death. (6)
Romeo's father (8)
Sends Romeo into exile (6)
Servant of the Capulets (6)
Servant to Romeo (9)
She refused Romeo's love and caused his depression. (8)
She wants the Prince to execute Romeo: ___ Capulet (4)
That which we call a _____ By any other name would smell as sweet. (4)
We are _____, lady, we are _____. (6)
What light through yonder _____ breaks? (6)
_____ is my son-in-law, _____ is my heir. (5)

Romeo & Juliet Word Search 2

Words are placed backwards, forward, diagonally, up and down. Clues listed below can help you find the words. Circle the hidden vocabulary words in the maze.

```
O R C H A R D N V G U Q D R O M E O C
J H Z Q H F O D E R N T E P J C W Z C
J G H J G S B K R I D B A L K J F L Q
W R Y K M R A C O E O D T D J X B P L
Z B D A V N L J N V N S H S O R R O W
P K S J M R T S A I E H D L E R K J B
L L L S O K H F X N B A L T C R F D J
L W L Y N Y A M R G N K C H N Y T P R
J I S Y T S S P J P L E M P E Q L N Z
V N Y P A V A F R P P S Z S R T G K G
V D F H G Q R T F O O P Y Z U I F M O
M O K O U Z L X D I S E D T A T N I Y
S W M F E U G A L P C A P U L E T C A
Z L Y R G N R O H A G R L A W U O R E
T G R O R B V B Q G D E B I C B M U E
P O I S O N S C E N E Y H R N H B T C
Y K T E E L C R G P T F E Q F E A C H
B Z L B J U L I E T Z M M K H F P H F
```

A _____ o'both your houses. (6)
A _____, a _____! Why call you for your sword? (6)
Act division (5)
Author William (11)
Both Paris and Romeo want to marry her. (6)
He agrees to marry Romeo & Juliet: Friar ___ (8)
He explains the circumstances of Tybalt's death. (8)
He gives a feast to introduce Juliet to bachelors. (7)
He is slain by Tybalt. (8)
He kills himself when he thinks Juliet is dead. (5)
Juliet kills herself with Romeo's (6)
Lady Montague dies ___ for her son, Romeo. (8)
Me thinks I see thee .... as one dead in the bottom of a _____. (4)
My life is my __'s debt. (3)
Paris is a nobleman from this place. (6)

Parting is such sweet _____. (6)
Play division (3)
Predestined future (4)
Romeo climbs over the wall surrounding Capulet's _____. (7)
Romeo drinks it and dies. (6)
Romeo kills him to avenge his friend's death. (6)
Romeo's father (8)
Sends Romeo into exile (6)
Servant of the Capulets (6)
Servant to Romeo (9)
She refused Romeo's love and caused his depression. (8)
She wants the Prince to execute Romeo: ___ Capulet (4)
That which we call a _____ By any other name would smell as sweet. (4)
We are _____, lady, we are _____. (6)
What light through yonder _____ breaks? (6)
_____ is my son-in-law, _____ is my heir. (5)

Romeo & Juliet Word Search 2 Answer Key

Words are placed backwards, forward, diagonally, up and down. Clues listed below can help you find the words. Circle the hidden vocabulary words in the maze.

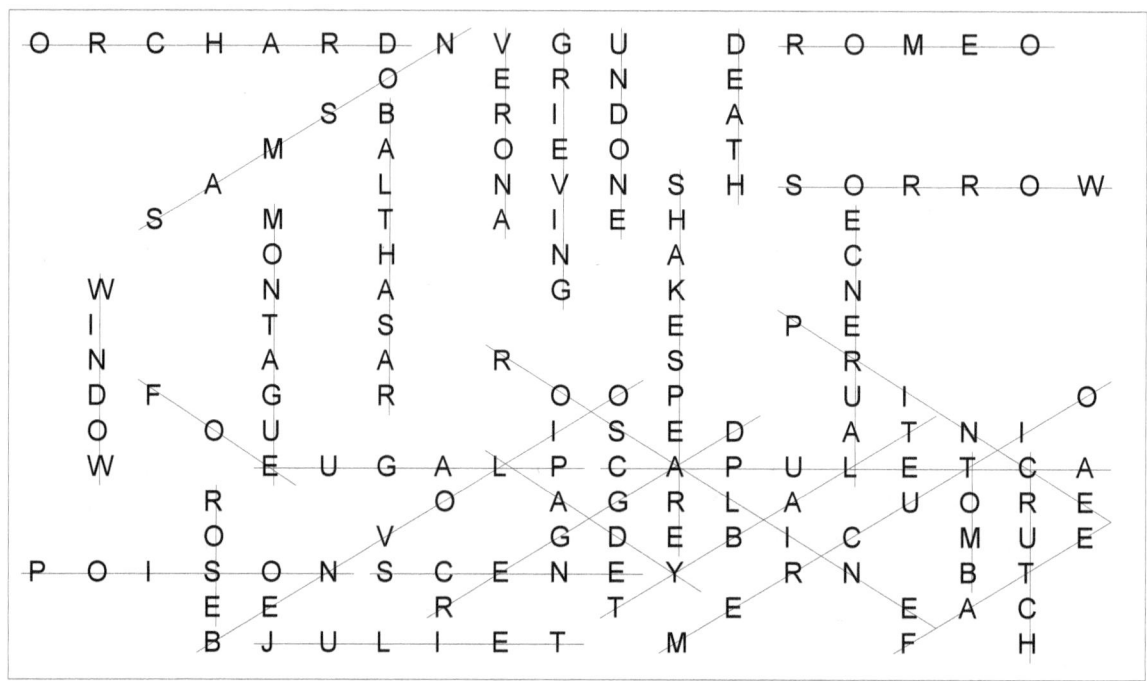

A ____ o'both your houses. (6)
A _____, a _____! Why call you for your sword? (6)
Act division (5)
Author William (11)
Both Paris and Romeo want to marry her. (6)
He agrees to marry Romeo & Juliet: Friar ___ (8)
He explains the circumstances of Tybalt's death. (8)
He gives a feast to introduce Juliet to bachelors. (7)
He is slain by Tybalt. (8)
He kills himself when he thinks Juliet is dead. (5)
Juliet kills herself with Romeo's (6)
Lady Montague dies ___ for her son, Romeo. (8)
Me thinks I see thee .... as one dead in the bottom of a _____. (4)
My life is my __'s debt. (3)
Paris is a nobleman from this place. (6)

Parting is such sweet _____. (6)
Play division (3)
Predestined future (4)
Romeo climbs over the wall surrounding Capulet's _____. (7)
Romeo drinks it and dies. (6)
Romeo kills him to avenge his friend's death. (6)
Romeo's father (8)
Sends Romeo into exile (6)
Servant of the Capulets (6)
Servant to Romeo (9)
She refused Romeo's love and caused his depression. (8)
She wants the Prince to execute Romeo: ___ Capulet (4)
That which we call a _____ By any other name would smell as sweet. (4)
We are _____, lady, we are _____. (6)
What light through yonder _____ breaks? (6)
_____ is my son-in-law, _____ is my heir. (5)

Romeo & Juliet Word Search 3

Words are placed backwards, forward, diagonally, up and down. Words listed below are included in the maze. Circle the hidden vocabulary words in the maze.

```
T Z M M Z X C F S F M Z T V C G Q H C
Z Q H O P V M K T V Z J D W P M L E M
R N B N S D G M S E F X B W M W N X R
P R K T F O B D V R W B E N V O L I O
Q O P A S C R D C O L H D R D D M N V
H S T G R B R R L N T A B N K N E E P
T E L U P A C N O A Z C U P R I N C E
T O T E H B O I E W D T D O O W E N K
W C M C G S T D N S K Y Z I M F C E J
H B R B M U J U L I E T D S E O S R B
C O C A C V R Z D R R M L O O E M U F
M F S R V Z M J A X O Z X N J Y B A N
D C E F T Q M P G G F S N Q X Q D L F
R M P L A G U E G T Y B A L T B N B T
K Z H M Y W Y C E Y W F S L B S F C S
B A L T H A S A R V V T L Z I Z T G G
S H A K E S P E A R E L N F R N Y M M
G R I E V I N G S K Z R T V C C E V T
```

ACT	FOE	PLAGUE	SHAKESPEARE
BALTHASAR	GRIEVING	POISON	SORROW
BENVOLIO	JULIET	PRINCE	TOMB
CAPULET	LADY	ROMEO	TYBALT
CRUTCH	LAURENCE	ROSALINE	UNDONE
DAGGER	MERCUTIO	ROSE	VERONA
DEATH	MONTAGUE	SAMSON	WINDOW
FATE	ORCHARD	SCENE	

Romeo & Juliet Word Search 3 Answer Key

Words are placed backwards, forward, diagonally, up and down. Words listed below are included in the maze. Circle the hidden vocabulary words in the maze.

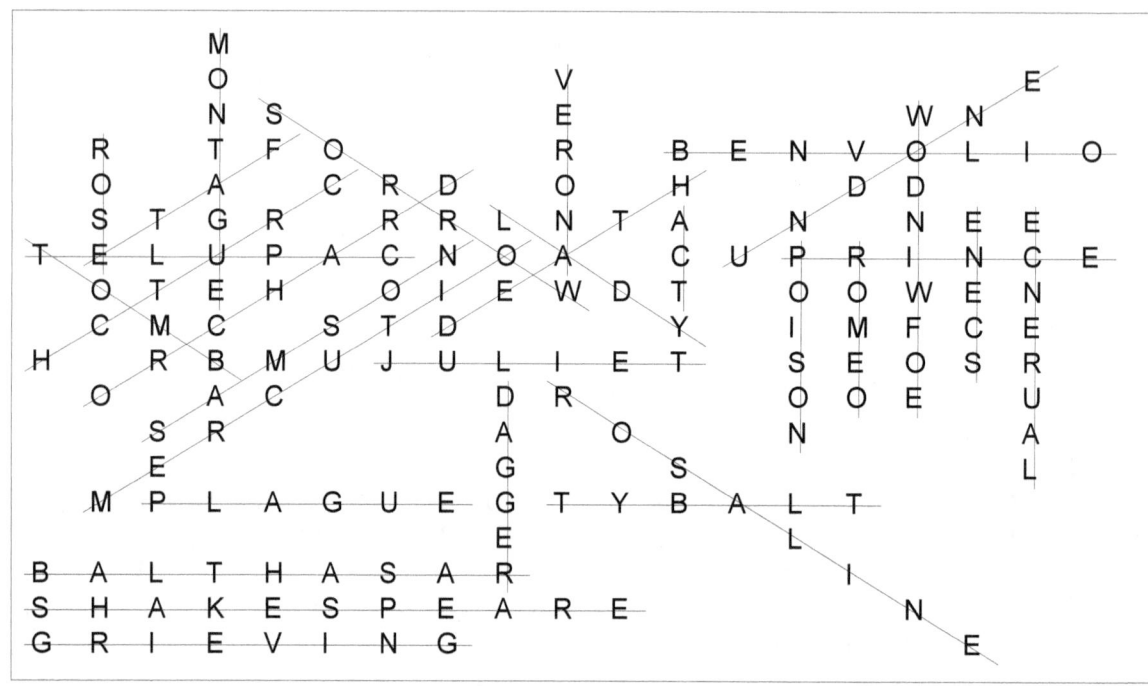

ACT	FOE	PLAGUE	SHAKESPEARE
BALTHASAR	GRIEVING	POISON	SORROW
BENVOLIO	JULIET	PRINCE	TOMB
CAPULET	LADY	ROMEO	TYBALT
CRUTCH	LAURENCE	ROSALINE	UNDONE
DAGGER	MERCUTIO	ROSE	VERONA
DEATH	MONTAGUE	SAMSON	WINDOW
FATE	ORCHARD	SCENE	

Romeo & Juliet Word Search 4

Words are placed backwards, forward, diagonally, up and down. Words listed below are included in the maze. Circle the hidden vocabulary words in the maze.

```
D Z M P M G V W S C V M H C K S W C F
H J G C P T J I F D E L T G E S E J G
K T N D L G W N Y X R D W G U U N C Y
T Q R A W B J D S S A M E Q G E I R X
M D D Q S U C O X E E Z M A A O L U F
T Y B A L T R W C A P U L E T F A T E
C H B I S W O N J H S P A N N H S C S
V Y E T H R I M Y N E O U E O M O H M
T T N X R R S D B G K R R C M T R B C
L N O O P A B L N B A C E S C W A E N
V S S G M Q M I M R H H N A D Y S N N
Y P I S S E V K L D S A C L T F A V B
E S O R V E R O N A P R E J W R H O T
N N P F I R O C D H X D B B E P T L H
O X B R X S M G U L G V T G K M L I G
D P G F G Y E L Z T R Z G T V D A O R
N D Q C L Q O F M V I A T S M T B D Q
U T Y D T V J Y T Y D O Y P S M X F D
```

ACT	FOE	PLAGUE	SHAKESPEARE
BALTHASAR	GRIEVING	POISON	SORROW
BENVOLIO	JULIET	PRINCE	TOMB
CAPULET	LADY	ROMEO	TYBALT
CRUTCH	LAURENCE	ROSALINE	UNDONE
DAGGER	MERCUTIO	ROSE	VERONA
DEATH	MONTAGUE	SAMSON	WINDOW
FATE	ORCHARD	SCENE	

Romeo & Juliet Word Search 4 Answer Key

Words are placed backwards, forward, diagonally, up and down. Words listed below are included in the maze. Circle the hidden vocabulary words in the maze.

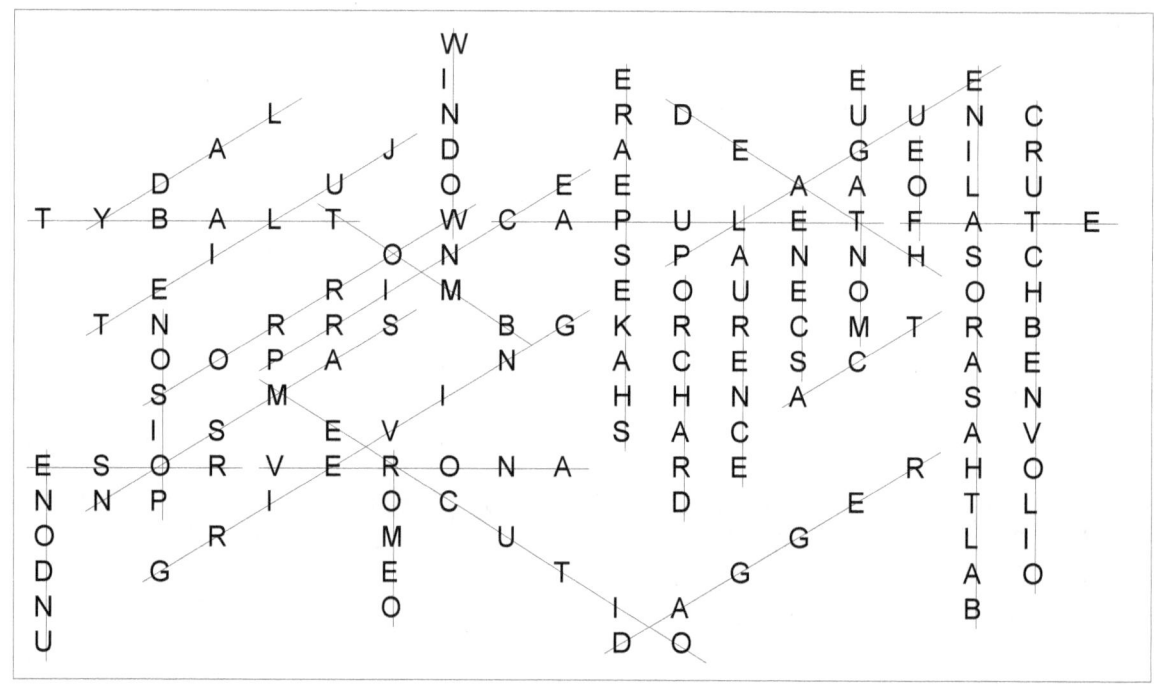

ACT	FOE	PLAGUE	SHAKESPEARE
BALTHASAR	GRIEVING	POISON	SORROW
BENVOLIO	JULIET	PRINCE	TOMB
CAPULET	LADY	ROMEO	TYBALT
CRUTCH	LAURENCE	ROSALINE	UNDONE
DAGGER	MERCUTIO	ROSE	VERONA
DEATH	MONTAGUE	SAMSON	WINDOW
FATE	ORCHARD	SCENE	

Romeo & Juliet Crossword 1

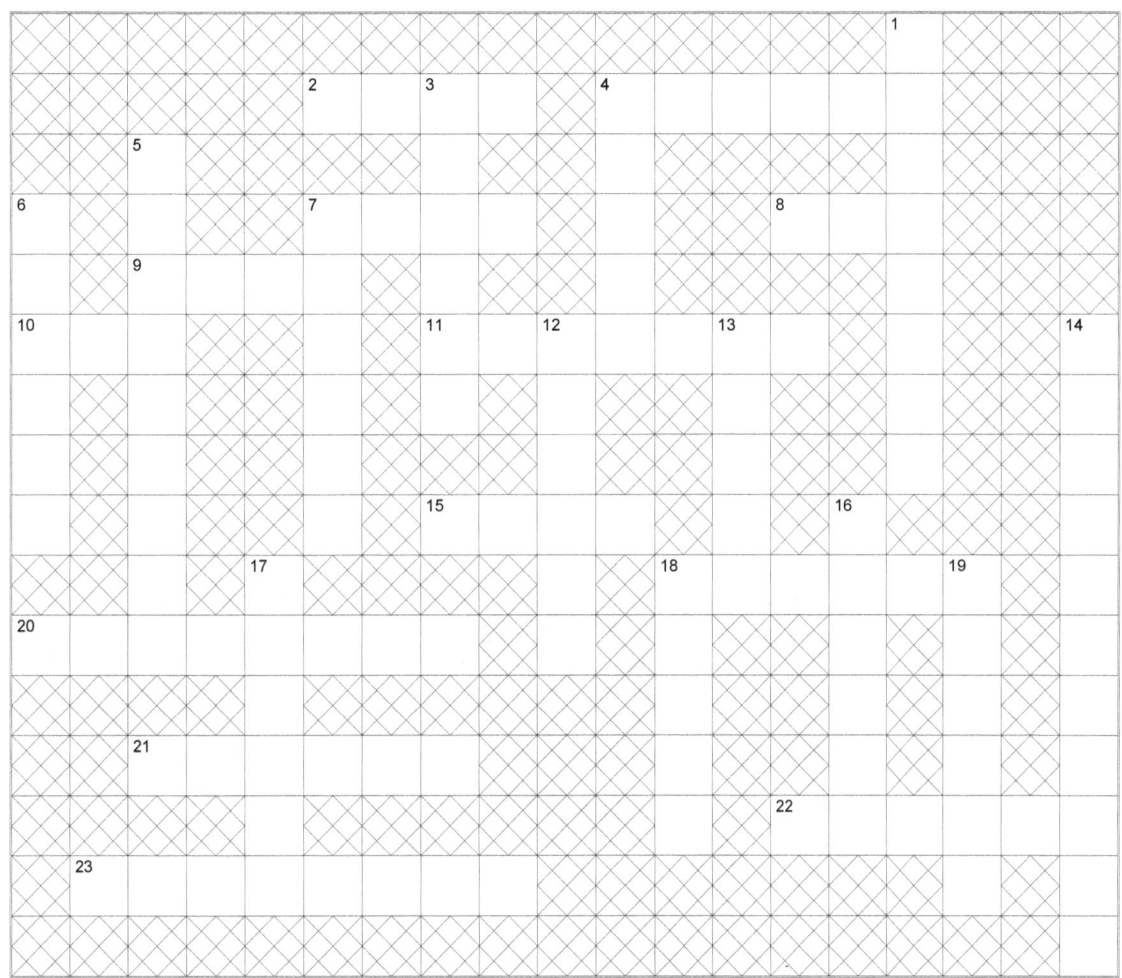

Across
2. That which we call a _____ By any other name would smell as sweet.
4. Juliet kills herself with Romeo's
7. Me thinks I see thee .... as one dead in the bottom of a _____.
8. My life is my __'s debt.
9. She wants the Prince to execute Romeo: ___ Capulet
10. Play division
11. Romeo climbs over the wall surrounding Capulet's _____.
15. Predestined future
18. Parting is such sweet _____.
20. He is slain by Tybalt.
21. Romeo drinks it and dies.
22. Paris is a nobleman from this place.
23. Romeo's father

Down
1. Lady Montague dies ___ for her son, Romeo.
3. Servant of the Capulets
4. _____ is my son-in-law, _____ is my heir.
5. Servant to Romeo
6. A ____ o'both your houses.
7. Romeo kills him to avenge his friend's death.
12. A _____, a _____! Why call you for your sword?
13. He kills himself when he thinks Juliet is dead.
14. Author William
16. Sends Romeo into exile
17. Both Paris and Romeo want to marry her.
18. Act division
19. What light through yonder _____ breaks?

Romeo & Juliet Crossword 1 Answer Key

										¹G	
		²R	³O	S	E	⁴D	A	G	G	E	R
	⁵B			A		E				I	
⁶P	A		⁷T	O	M	B	A		⁸F	O	E
L	⁹L	A	D	Y		S			T		V
¹⁰A	C	T		¹¹B	¹²O	R	C	¹³H	A	R	D		¹⁴S
G	H			A	N		R		O		I		H
U	A			L			U		M		N		A
E	S			T		¹⁵F	A	T	E		¹⁶P		K
	¹⁷A						C		¹⁸S	O	R	¹⁹R	O	W	E
²⁰M	E	R	C	U	T	I	O		H		C		I		I	S
		L							E		N		N		P
	²¹P	O	I	S	O	N			N		C		D	E
		E							E		²²V	E	R	O	N	A
	²³M	O	N	T	A	G	U	E					W		R
															E

Across
2. That which we call a _____ By any other name would smell as sweet.
4. Juliet kills herself with Romeo's
7. Me thinks I see thee .... as one dead in the bottom of a _____.
8. My life is my __'s debt.
9. She wants the Prince to execute Romeo: ___ Capulet
10. Play division
11. Romeo climbs over the wall surrounding Capulet's _____.
15. Predestined future
18. Parting is such sweet _____.
20. He is slain by Tybalt.
21. Romeo drinks it and dies.
22. Paris is a nobleman from this place.
23. Romeo's father

Down
1. Lady Montague dies ___ for her son, Romeo.
3. Servant of the Capulets
4. _____ is my son-in-law, _____ is my heir.
5. Servant to Romeo
6. A ____ o'both your houses.
7. Romeo kills him to avenge his friend's death.
12. A _____, a _____! Why call you for your sword?
13. He kills himself when he thinks Juliet is dead.
14. Author William
16. Sends Romeo into exile
17. Both Paris and Romeo want to marry her.
18. Act division
19. What light through yonder _____ breaks?

Romeo & Juliet Crossword 2

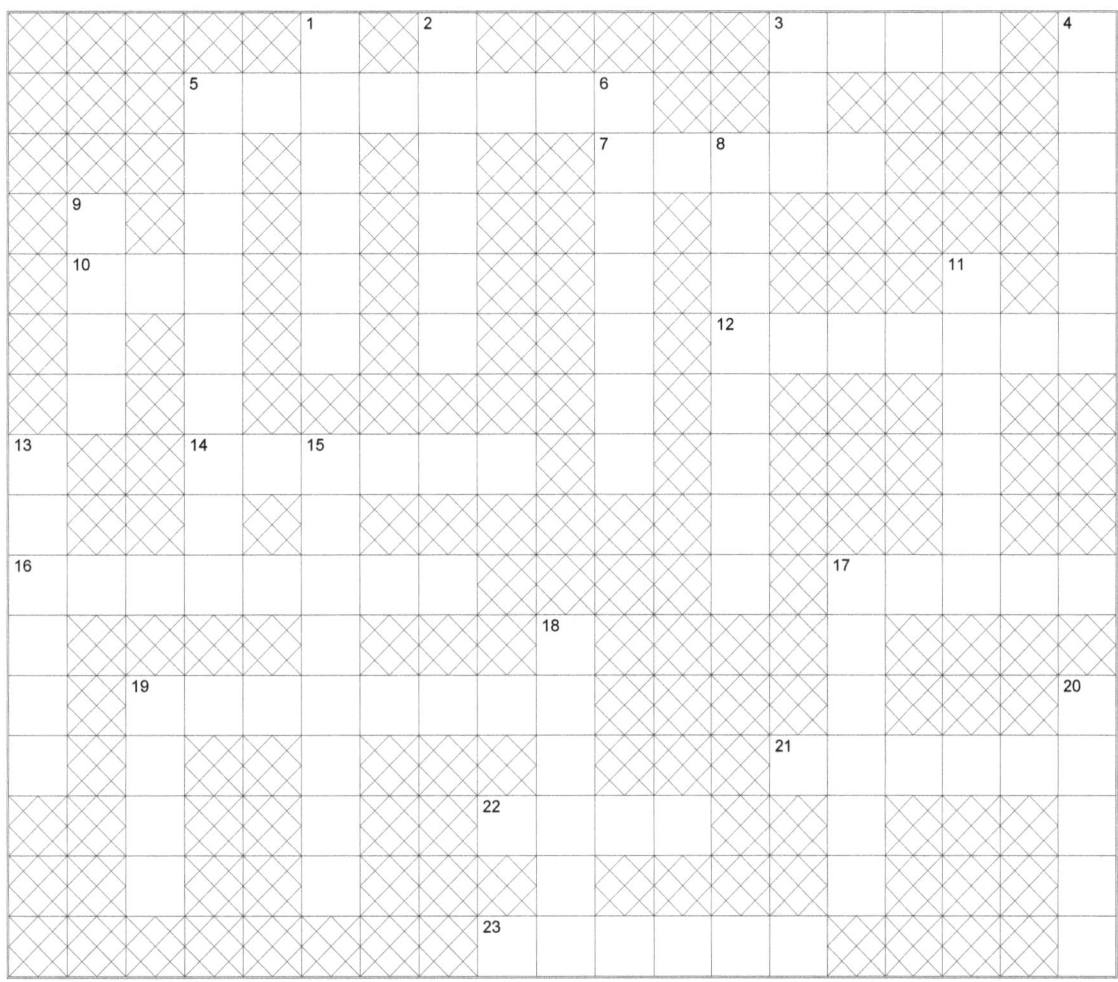

Across
3. Predestined future
5. He explains the circumstances of Tybalt's death.
7. He kills himself when he thinks Juliet is dead.
10. Play division
12. He gives a feast to introduce Juliet to bachelors.
14. Servant of the Capulets
16. He agrees to marry Romeo & Juliet: Friar ___
17. Act division
19. She refused Romeo's love and caused his depression.
21. Sends Romeo into exile
22. Me thinks I see thee .... as one dead in the bottom of a _____.
23. Juliet kills herself with Romeo's

Down
1. We are _____, lady, we are _____.
2. Romeo drinks it and dies.
3. My life is my __'s debt.
4. Romeo kills him to avenge his friend's death.
5. Servant to Romeo
6. Romeo climbs over the wall surrounding Capulet's _____.
8. He is slain by Tybalt.
9. She wants the Prince to execute Romeo: ___ Capulet
11. A ____ o'both your houses.
13. Both Paris and Romeo want to marry her.
15. Romeo's father
17. Parting is such sweet _____.
18. Paris is a nobleman from this place.
19. That which we call a _____ By any other name would smell as sweet.
20. _____ is my son-in-law, _____ is my heir.

Romeo & Juliet Crossword 2 Answer Key

	1		2			3 F	A	T	E		4 T
	U		P								Y
5 B	E	N	V	O	L	I	O		O		B
A		D				7 R	O	8 M	E	O	
9 L	L		O		S		C		E			A
10 A	C	T		N		O		H		R		11 P	L
D		H		E		N		A	12 C	A	P	U	L	E	T
Y		A						R		U			A		
13 J	14 S	A	15 M	S	O	N		D		T			G		
U		A		O						I			U		
16 L	A	U	R	E	N	C	E			O		17 S	C	E	N	E
I			T				18 V					O			
E	19 R	O	S	A	L	I	N	E				R		20 D
T		O				G		R		21 P	R	I	N	C	E
			S			U	22 T	O	M	B		O			A
			E			E	N					W			T
							23 D	A	G	G	E	R			H

Across

3. Predestined future
5. He explains the circumstances of Tybalt's death.
7. He kills himself when he thinks Juliet is dead.
10. Play division
12. He gives a feast to introduce Juliet to bachelors.
14. Servant of the Capulets
16. He agrees to marry Romeo & Juliet: Friar ___
17. Act division
19. She refused Romeo's love and caused his depression.
21. Sends Romeo into exile
22. Me thinks I see thee .... as one dead in the bottom of a _____.
23. Juliet kills herself with Romeo's

Down

1. We are _____, lady, we are _____.
2. Romeo drinks it and dies.
3. My life is my __'s debt.
4. Romeo kills him to avenge his friend's death.
5. Servant to Romeo
6. Romeo climbs over the wall surrounding Capulet's _____.
8. He is slain by Tybalt.
9. She wants the Prince to execute Romeo: ___ Capulet
11. A ____ o'both your houses.
13. Both Paris and Romeo want to marry her.
15. Romeo's father
17. Parting is such sweet _____.
18. Paris is a nobleman from this place.
19. That which we call a _____ By any other name would smell as sweet.
20. _____ is my son-in-law, _____ is my heir.

Romeo & Juliet Crossword 3

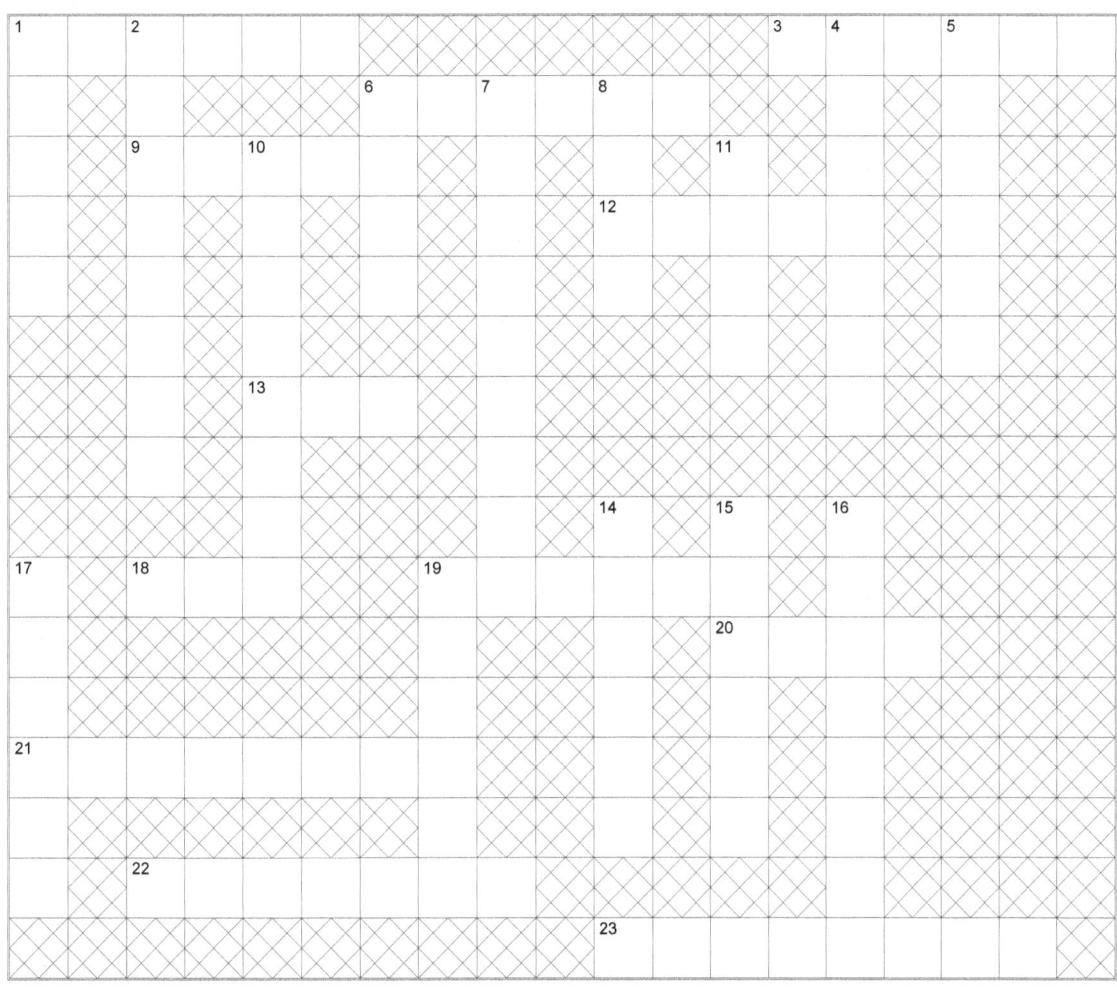

Across
1. Servant of the Capulets
3. Romeo drinks it and dies.
6. Romeo kills him to avenge his friend's death.
9. He kills himself when he thinks Juliet is dead.
12. _____ is my son-in-law, _____ is my heir.
13. Play division
18. My life is my __'s debt.
19. Sends Romeo into exile
20. That which we call a _____ By any other name would smell as sweet.
21. Lady Montague dies ___ for her son, Romeo.
22. He gives a feast to introduce Juliet to bachelors.
23. He agrees to marry Romeo & Juliet: Friar ___

Down
1. Act division
2. He is slain by Tybalt.
4. Romeo climbs over the wall surrounding Capulet's _____.
5. Parting is such sweet _____.
6. Me thinks I see thee .... as one dead in the bottom of a _____.
7. Servant to Romeo
8. She wants the Prince to execute Romeo: ___ Capulet
10. Romeo's father
11. Predestined future
14. We are _____, lady, we are _____.
15. Paris is a nobleman from this place.
16. She refused Romeo's love and caused his depression.
17. Juliet kills herself with Romeo's ___
19. A ____ o'both your houses.

Romeo & Juliet Crossword 3 Answer Key

	1 S	A	2 M	S	O	N					3 P	4 O	I	5 S	O	N
	C		E				6 T	7 Y	B	8 A	L	T		R		O
	E		9 R	10 O	M	E	O		A	L	11 F		C		O	
	N		C	O		M			L	12 D	E	A	T	H		R
	E		U	N		B			T	Y		T		A		O
			T	T					H			E		R		W
			I	13 A	C	T			A					D		
			O	G					S							
				U					A		14 U	15 V		16 R		
	17 D	18 F	O	E				19 P	R	I	N	C	E	O		
	A							L			D	20 R	O	S	E	
	G							A			O	O		A		
	21 G	R	I	E	V	I	N	G			N	N		L		
	E							U			E	A		I		
	R		22 C	A	P	U	L	E	T					N		
								23 L	A	U	R	E	N	C	E	

Across
1. Servant of the Capulets
3. Romeo drinks it and dies.
6. Romeo kills him to avenge his friend's death.
9. He kills himself when he thinks Juliet is dead.
12. _____ is my son-in-law, _____ is my heir.
13. Play division
18. My life is my __'s debt.
19. Sends Romeo into exile
20. That which we call a _____ By any other name would smell as sweet.
21. Lady Montague dies ___ for her son, Romeo.
22. He gives a feast to introduce Juliet to bachelors.
23. He agrees to marry Romeo & Juliet: Friar ___

Down
1. Act division
2. He is slain by Tybalt.
4. Romeo climbs over the wall surrounding Capulet's _____.
5. Parting is such sweet _____.
6. Me thinks I see thee .... as one dead in the bottom of a _____.
7. Servant to Romeo
8. She wants the Prince to execute Romeo: ___ Capulet
10. Romeo's father
11. Predestined future
14. We are _____, lady, we are _____.
15. Paris is a nobleman from this place.
16. She refused Romeo's love and caused his depression.
17. Juliet kills herself with Romeo's
19. A ____ o'both your houses.

Romeo & Juliet Crossword 4

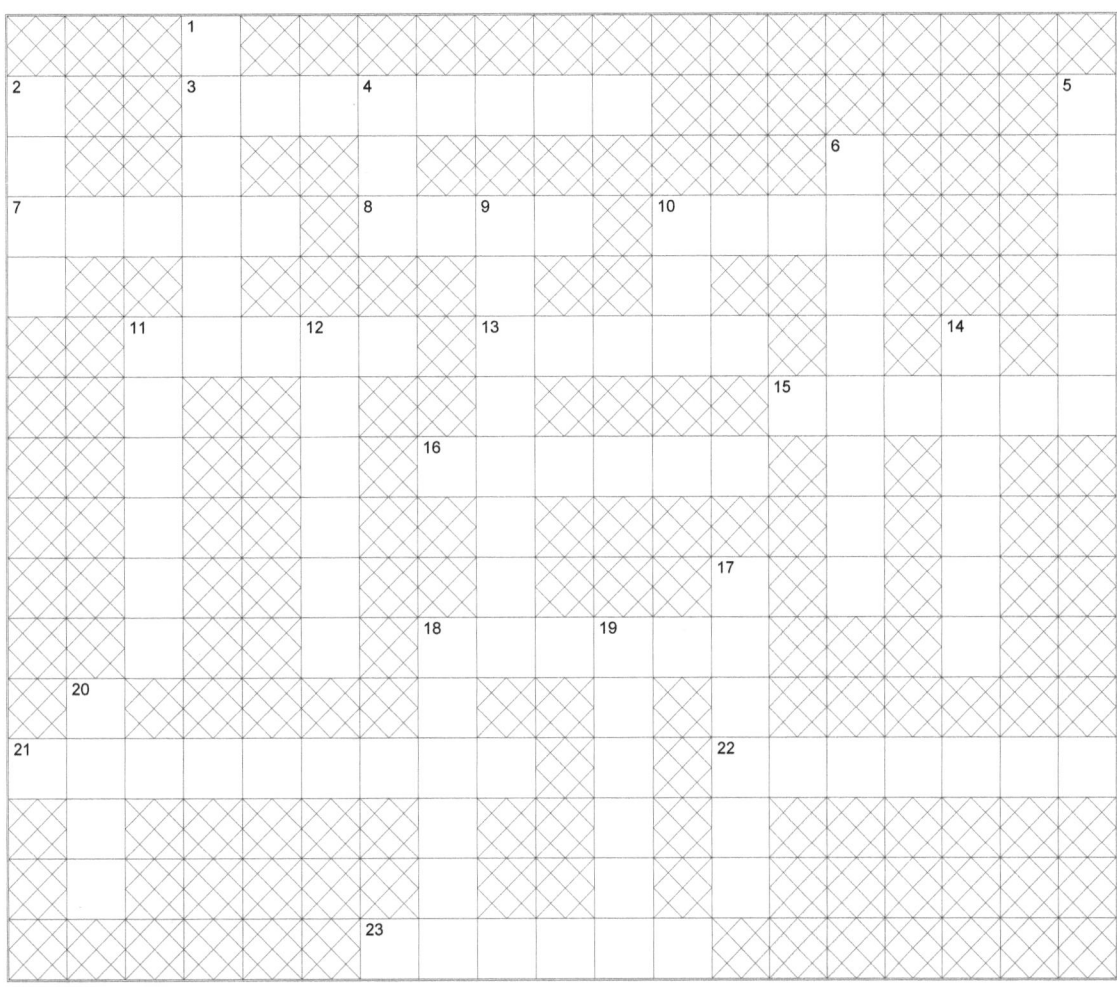

Across

3. She refused Romeo's love and caused his depression.
7. Act division
8. Me thinks I see thee .... as one dead in the bottom of a _____.
10. Predestined future
11. _____ is my son-in-law, _____ is my heir.
13. He kills himself when he thinks Juliet is dead.
15. Parting is such sweet _____.
16. Both Paris and Romeo want to marry her.
18. Romeo drinks it and dies.
21. Servant to Romeo
22. Romeo climbs over the wall surrounding Capulet's _____.
23. Paris is a nobleman from this place.

Down

1. Sends Romeo into exile
2. That which we call a _____ By any other name would smell as sweet.
4. Play division
5. What light through yonder _____ breaks?
6. He explains the circumstances of Tybalt's death.
9. He is slain by Tybalt.
10. My life is my __'s debt.
11. Juliet kills herself with Romeo's
12. Romeo kills him to avenge his friend's death.
14. A _____, a _____! Why call you for your sword?
17. We are _____, lady, we are _____.
18. A ____ o'both your houses.
19. Servant of the Capulets
20. She wants the Prince to execute Romeo: ___ Capulet

Romeo & Juliet Crossword 4 Answer Key

			¹P									
²R		³R	O	S	⁴A	L	I	N	E			⁵W
O		I			C					⁶B		I
⁷S	C	E	N	E	⁸T	O	⁹M	B	¹⁰F	A	T	E
E		C			O		E		O		N		D
		¹¹D	E	A	¹²T	H	¹³R	O	M	E	O	¹⁴C	O
		A			Y		C			¹⁵S	O	R	R	O	W
		G			B		¹⁶J	U	L	I	E	T	
		G			A		T			L		U	
		E			L		I		¹⁷U		O		C
		R			T		¹⁸P	O	I	¹⁹S	O	N		H
	²⁰L						L		A		D		
²¹B	A	L	T	H	A	S	A	R		M		²²O	R	C	H	A	R	D
	D						G			S		N		
	Y						U			O		E		
					²³V	E	R	O	N	A				

Across
3. She refused Romeo's love and caused his depression.
7. Act division
8. Me thinks I see thee .... as one dead in the bottom of a _____.
10. Predestined future
11. _____ is my son-in-law, _____ is my heir.
13. He kills himself when he thinks Juliet is dead.
15. Parting is such sweet _____.
16. Both Paris and Romeo want to marry her.
18. Romeo drinks it and dies.
21. Servant to Romeo
22. Romeo climbs over the wall surrounding Capulet's _____.
23. Paris is a nobleman from this place.

Down
1. Sends Romeo into exile
2. That which we call a _____ By any other name would smell as sweet.
4. Play division
5. What light through yonder _____ breaks?
6. He explains the circumstances of Tybalt's death.
9. He is slain by Tybalt.
10. My life is my __'s debt.
11. Juliet kills herself with Romeo's
12. Romeo kills him to avenge his friend's death.
14. A _____, a _____! Why call you for your sword?
17. We are _____, lady, we are _____.
18. A ____ o'both your houses.
19. Servant of the Capulets
20. She wants the Prince to execute Romeo: ___ Capulet

44
Copyrighted

Romeo & Juliet

SORROW	WINDOW	BALTHASAR	FOE	ACT
CAPULET	PLAGUE	MERCUTIO	ROMEO	POISON
UNDONE	TYBALT	FREE SPACE	DAGGER	VERONA
ROSALINE	PRINCE	CRUTCH	ROSE	JULIET
SHAKESPEARE	SAMSON	SCENE	LADY	GRIEVING

Romeo & Juliet

FATE	TOMB	DEATH	LAURENCE	BENVOLIO
ORCHARD	GRIEVING	LADY	SCENE	SAMSON
SHAKESPEARE	JULIET	FREE SPACE	CRUTCH	PRINCE
ROSALINE	VERONA	DAGGER	MONTAGUE	TYBALT
UNDONE	POISON	ROMEO	MERCUTIO	PLAGUE

Romeo & Juliet

DEATH	LADY	FATE	CRUTCH	SAMSON
WINDOW	ROSE	LAURENCE	PLAGUE	DAGGER
VERONA	PRINCE	FREE SPACE	JULIET	SHAKESPEARE
TOMB	UNDONE	POISON	ROMEO	FOE
GRIEVING	MERCUTIO	BENVOLIO	BALTHASAR	ORCHARD

Romeo & Juliet

MONTAGUE	ROSALINE	SCENE	SORROW	TYBALT
ACT	ORCHARD	BALTHASAR	BENVOLIO	MERCUTIO
GRIEVING	FOE	FREE SPACE	POISON	UNDONE
TOMB	SHAKESPEARE	JULIET	CAPULET	PRINCE
VERONA	DAGGER	PLAGUE	LAURENCE	ROSE

Romeo & Juliet

FOE	TOMB	LAURENCE	VERONA	SAMSON
DAGGER	POISON	SCENE	FATE	JULIET
PLAGUE	MONTAGUE	FREE SPACE	DEATH	ROMEO
MERCUTIO	UNDONE	SHAKESPEARE	ROSALINE	CRUTCH
BALTHASAR	ACT	GRIEVING	ROSE	CAPULET

Romeo & Juliet

TYBALT	LADY	WINDOW	ORCHARD	BENVOLIO
PRINCE	CAPULET	ROSE	GRIEVING	ACT
BALTHASAR	CRUTCH	FREE SPACE	SHAKESPEARE	UNDONE
MERCUTIO	ROMEO	DEATH	SORROW	MONTAGUE
PLAGUE	JULIET	FATE	SCENE	POISON

Romeo & Juliet

MONTAGUE	DAGGER	UNDONE	BALTHASAR	DEATH
PRINCE	JULIET	CRUTCH	SCENE	ROSE
ACT	WINDOW	FREE SPACE	LADY	ROMEO
TOMB	SHAKESPEARE	TYBALT	PLAGUE	SAMSON
FATE	SORROW	ROSALINE	ORCHARD	GRIEVING

Romeo & Juliet

BENVOLIO	POISON	CAPULET	MERCUTIO	FOE
VERONA	GRIEVING	ORCHARD	ROSALINE	SORROW
FATE	SAMSON	FREE SPACE	TYBALT	SHAKESPEARE
TOMB	ROMEO	LADY	LAURENCE	WINDOW
ACT	ROSE	SCENE	CRUTCH	JULIET

Romeo & Juliet

DAGGER	CRUTCH	TYBALT	WINDOW	PRINCE
DEATH	ROSALINE	FATE	VERONA	GRIEVING
CAPULET	FOE	FREE SPACE	UNDONE	SCENE
JULIET	PLAGUE	ROSE	MERCUTIO	LADY
BALTHASAR	SORROW	LAURENCE	ORCHARD	SAMSON

Romeo & Juliet

MONTAGUE	ROMEO	POISON	SHAKESPEARE	ACT
BENVOLIO	SAMSON	ORCHARD	LAURENCE	SORROW
BALTHASAR	LADY	FREE SPACE	ROSE	PLAGUE
JULIET	SCENE	UNDONE	TOMB	FOE
CAPULET	GRIEVING	VERONA	FATE	ROSALINE

Romeo & Juliet

MERCUTIO	MONTAGUE	SAMSON	FATE	FOE
JULIET	BALTHASAR	LADY	TYBALT	SCENE
ROSE	TOMB	FREE SPACE	VERONA	UNDONE
ROSALINE	POISON	ORCHARD	DAGGER	ACT
WINDOW	DEATH	GRIEVING	LAURENCE	SORROW

Romeo & Juliet

CRUTCH	PLAGUE	CAPULET	BENVOLIO	PRINCE
ROMEO	SORROW	LAURENCE	GRIEVING	DEATH
WINDOW	ACT	FREE SPACE	ORCHARD	POISON
ROSALINE	UNDONE	VERONA	SHAKESPEARE	TOMB
ROSE	SCENE	TYBALT	LADY	BALTHASAR

Romeo & Juliet

BENVOLIO	ACT	WINDOW	FATE	TOMB
GRIEVING	POISON	PRINCE	ROSE	JULIET
LAURENCE	DEATH	FREE SPACE	ROSALINE	UNDONE
LADY	SCENE	CAPULET	PLAGUE	MERCUTIO
MONTAGUE	DAGGER	SORROW	SAMSON	BALTHASAR

Romeo & Juliet

VERONA	ROMEO	CRUTCH	FOE	TYBALT
ORCHARD	BALTHASAR	SAMSON	SORROW	DAGGER
MONTAGUE	MERCUTIO	FREE SPACE	CAPULET	SCENE
LADY	UNDONE	ROSALINE	SHAKESPEARE	DEATH
LAURENCE	JULIET	ROSE	PRINCE	POISON

Romeo & Juliet

FATE	BALTHASAR	PRINCE	GRIEVING	ORCHARD
ACT	VERONA	TOMB	LAURENCE	ROMEO
PLAGUE	FOE	FREE SPACE	CAPULET	DEATH
ROSALINE	CRUTCH	JULIET	SHAKESPEARE	UNDONE
MONTAGUE	BENVOLIO	TYBALT	SCENE	LADY

Romeo & Juliet

SAMSON	ROSE	DAGGER	POISON	MERCUTIO
SORROW	LADY	SCENE	TYBALT	BENVOLIO
MONTAGUE	UNDONE	FREE SPACE	JULIET	CRUTCH
ROSALINE	DEATH	CAPULET	WINDOW	FOE
PLAGUE	ROMEO	LAURENCE	TOMB	VERONA

Romeo & Juliet

DAGGER	ACT	ROSALINE	CRUTCH	PRINCE
FATE	CAPULET	GRIEVING	SHAKESPEARE	PLAGUE
SAMSON	ROMEO	FREE SPACE	LAURENCE	DEATH
MONTAGUE	FOE	BENVOLIO	POISON	JULIET
ROSE	BALTHASAR	ORCHARD	LADY	SCENE

Romeo & Juliet

VERONA	TOMB	TYBALT	MERCUTIO	UNDONE
SORROW	SCENE	LADY	ORCHARD	BALTHASAR
ROSE	JULIET	FREE SPACE	BENVOLIO	FOE
MONTAGUE	DEATH	LAURENCE	WINDOW	ROMEO
SAMSON	PLAGUE	SHAKESPEARE	GRIEVING	CAPULET

Romeo & Juliet

LAURENCE	DAGGER	TYBALT	CAPULET	WINDOW
DEATH	FOE	CRUTCH	FATE	SAMSON
ACT	MERCUTIO	FREE SPACE	SCENE	UNDONE
ROSALINE	BALTHASAR	BENVOLIO	ROSE	MONTAGUE
VERONA	PRINCE	LADY	TOMB	SORROW

Romeo & Juliet

ROMEO	JULIET	ORCHARD	POISON	GRIEVING
SHAKESPEARE	SORROW	TOMB	LADY	PRINCE
VERONA	MONTAGUE	FREE SPACE	BENVOLIO	BALTHASAR
ROSALINE	UNDONE	SCENE	PLAGUE	MERCUTIO
ACT	SAMSON	FATE	CRUTCH	FOE

Romeo & Juliet

ROSALINE	SCENE	PRINCE	PLAGUE	CRUTCH
VERONA	GRIEVING	SORROW	JULIET	LADY
ROSE	BALTHASAR	FREE SPACE	POISON	SHAKESPEARE
LAURENCE	DEATH	CAPULET	FOE	FATE
MONTAGUE	TYBALT	ORCHARD	MERCUTIO	TOMB

Romeo & Juliet

BENVOLIO	UNDONE	ROMEO	WINDOW	SAMSON
ACT	TOMB	MERCUTIO	ORCHARD	TYBALT
MONTAGUE	FATE	FREE SPACE	CAPULET	DEATH
LAURENCE	SHAKESPEARE	POISON	DAGGER	BALTHASAR
ROSE	LADY	JULIET	SORROW	GRIEVING

Romeo & Juliet

SHAKESPEARE	TOMB	ORCHARD	MONTAGUE	DEATH
CAPULET	ROMEO	UNDONE	CRUTCH	VERONA
LAURENCE	ACT	FREE SPACE	PRINCE	MERCUTIO
LADY	SCENE	WINDOW	POISON	JULIET
DAGGER	BALTHASAR	GRIEVING	ROSALINE	FATE

Romeo & Juliet

BENVOLIO	SAMSON	TYBALT	ROSE	PLAGUE
SORROW	FATE	ROSALINE	GRIEVING	BALTHASAR
DAGGER	JULIET	FREE SPACE	WINDOW	SCENE
LADY	MERCUTIO	PRINCE	FOE	ACT
LAURENCE	VERONA	CRUTCH	UNDONE	ROMEO

Romeo & Juliet

VERONA	DAGGER	ORCHARD	FOE	LADY
FATE	BENVOLIO	LAURENCE	SHAKESPEARE	JULIET
MONTAGUE	ROSE	FREE SPACE	SAMSON	MERCUTIO
ROMEO	TYBALT	POISON	UNDONE	SORROW
SCENE	TOMB	DEATH	ROSALINE	CRUTCH

Romeo & Juliet

CAPULET	WINDOW	PRINCE	GRIEVING	ACT
PLAGUE	CRUTCH	ROSALINE	DEATH	TOMB
SCENE	SORROW	FREE SPACE	POISON	TYBALT
ROMEO	MERCUTIO	SAMSON	BALTHASAR	ROSE
MONTAGUE	JULIET	SHAKESPEARE	LAURENCE	BENVOLIO

Romeo & Juliet

CAPULET	SAMSON	ORCHARD	VERONA	BENVOLIO
ROMEO	BALTHASAR	TOMB	LADY	LAURENCE
DEATH	TYBALT	FREE SPACE	POISON	GRIEVING
MONTAGUE	ACT	ROSALINE	FOE	DAGGER
MERCUTIO	PLAGUE	SCENE	SHAKESPEARE	WINDOW

Romeo & Juliet

FATE	ROSE	SORROW	CRUTCH	UNDONE
PRINCE	WINDOW	SHAKESPEARE	SCENE	PLAGUE
MERCUTIO	DAGGER	FREE SPACE	ROSALINE	ACT
MONTAGUE	GRIEVING	POISON	JULIET	TYBALT
DEATH	LAURENCE	LADY	TOMB	BALTHASAR

Romeo & Juliet

ROSALINE	ROMEO	UNDONE	CRUTCH	TOMB
DEATH	FATE	DAGGER	MONTAGUE	SAMSON
JULIET	ACT	FREE SPACE	FOE	ORCHARD
LAURENCE	ROSE	CAPULET	BALTHASAR	SCENE
POISON	SHAKESPEARE	PLAGUE	VERONA	TYBALT

Romeo & Juliet

MERCUTIO	GRIEVING	BENVOLIO	LADY	PRINCE
WINDOW	TYBALT	VERONA	PLAGUE	SHAKESPEARE
POISON	SCENE	FREE SPACE	CAPULET	ROSE
LAURENCE	ORCHARD	FOE	SORROW	ACT
JULIET	SAMSON	MONTAGUE	DAGGER	FATE

Romeo & Juliet

LAURENCE	VERONA	GRIEVING	UNDONE	CRUTCH
LADY	BALTHASAR	MONTAGUE	ROMEO	ORCHARD
SAMSON	FATE	FREE SPACE	TYBALT	BENVOLIO
ROSE	MERCUTIO	ROSALINE	DEATH	SHAKESPEARE
ACT	PRINCE	POISON	SCENE	FOE

Romeo & Juliet

DAGGER	JULIET	WINDOW	CAPULET	TOMB
PLAGUE	FOE	SCENE	POISON	PRINCE
ACT	SHAKESPEARE	FREE SPACE	ROSALINE	MERCUTIO
ROSE	BENVOLIO	TYBALT	SORROW	FATE
SAMSON	ORCHARD	ROMEO	MONTAGUE	BALTHASAR

Romeo and Juliet Vocabulary Word List

No.	Word	Clue/Definition
1.	ALDERMAN	A member of the municipal legislative body
2.	APPERTAINING	Belonging to as a proper function or part
3.	ARBITRATING	Negotiating differences through an impartial third party
4.	AUGMENTING	Making something already developed greater
5.	BEGUILED	Deceived by guile
6.	BENEFICE	A church office endowed with fixed capital assets
7.	BESEECH	Request earnestly
8.	BOISTEROUS	Rough and stormy; noisy and excited
9.	CHIDE	Express disapproval
10.	CONSORT	A companion or partner
11.	CULLED	Gathered; collected
12.	DIRGE	Funeral hymn or lament
13.	DISCOURSE	Narrate or discuss
14.	ENMITY	Deep seated, often mutual hatred
15.	ENVIOUS	Jealous
16.	ESTEEM	Regard with respect
17.	HERETIC	Person who holds opinions contrary to the beliefs of others in a group
18.	IMPEACH	Challenge the validity of something
19.	IMPUTE	To attribute; to credit
20.	INUNDATION	Covering with water; a swamping
21.	INVOCATION	Incantation used in conjuring
22.	LAMENTABLE	Causing grief
23.	LANGUISH	Be or become weak or feeble
24.	LOATHED	Disliked
25.	MANTLE	Cloak; coat
26.	OBSCURED	Indistinctly heard; partially hidden from the senses
27.	ORISONS	Prayers
28.	PENURY	Destitution
29.	PERNICIOUS	Evil; wicked
30.	PORTENTOUS	Foreboding
31.	POSTERITY	Future generations
32.	POULTICE	A soft, moist mass of bread, meal or clay
33.	PREDOMINANT	Most common or conspicuous
34.	PRESAGE	An omen
35.	PROFANERS	Those showing irreverence for what is sacred
36.	PROROGUE	Discontinue a session
37.	PURGED	Freed from impurities
38.	RANCOR	Bitterness
39.	SOLACE	Comfort in sorrow
40.	TEDIOUS	Moving or progressing very slowly
41.	TRANSGRESSION	Violation of a law
42.	VALIDITY	Good health; how sound something is

Romeo and Juliet Vocabulary Fill In The Blanks 1

_____ 1. Request earnestly

_____ 2. Cloak; coat

_____ 3. Funeral hymn or lament

_____ 4. Those showing irreverence for what is sacred

_____ 5. Person who holds opinions contrary to the beliefs of others in a group

_____ 6. Bitterness

_____ 7. A church office endowed with fixed capital assets

_____ 8. Belonging to as a proper function or part

_____ 9. Express disapproval

_____ 10. A soft, moist mass of bread, meal or clay

_____ 11. Rough and stormy; noisy and excited

_____ 12. Discontinue a session

_____ 13. Be or become weak or feeble

_____ 14. Moving or progressing very slowly

_____ 15. Incantation used in conjuring

_____ 16. Narrate or discuss

_____ 17. Evil; wicked

_____ 18. Good health; how sound something is

_____ 19. Jealous

_____ 20. Negotiating differences through an impartial third party

Romeo and Juliet Vocabulary Fill In The Blanks 1 Answer Key

BESEECH	1.	Request earnestly
MANTLE	2.	Cloak; coat
DIRGE	3.	Funeral hymn or lament
PROFANERS	4.	Those showing irreverence for what is sacred
HERETIC	5.	Person who holds opinions contrary to the beliefs of others in a group
RANCOR	6.	Bitterness
BENEFICE	7.	A church office endowed with fixed capital assets
APPERTAINING	8.	Belonging to as a proper function or part
CHIDE	9.	Express disapproval
POULTICE	10.	A soft, moist mass of bread, meal or clay
BOISTEROUS	11.	Rough and stormy; noisy and excited
PROROGUE	12.	Discontinue a session
LANGUISH	13.	Be or become weak or feeble
TEDIOUS	14.	Moving or progressing very slowly
INVOCATION	15.	Incantation used in conjuring
DISCOURSE	16.	Narrate or discuss
PERNICIOUS	17.	Evil; wicked
VALIDITY	18.	Good health; how sound something is
ENVIOUS	19.	Jealous
ARBITRATING	20.	Negotiating differences through an impartial third party

Romeo and Juliet Vocabulary Fill In The Blanks 2

_____ 1. Prayers

_____ 2. Most common or conspicuous

_____ 3. Violation of a law

_____ 4. Indistinctly heard; partially hidden from the senses

_____ 5. Those showing irreverence for what is sacred

_____ 6. Discontinue a session

_____ 7. Future generations

_____ 8. Moving or progressing very slowly

_____ 9. Covering with water; a swamping

_____ 10. Rough and stormy; noisy and excited

_____ 11. Good health; how sound something is

_____ 12. A member of the municipal legislative body

_____ 13. Destitution

_____ 14. Disliked

_____ 15. An omen

_____ 16. Regard with respect

_____ 17. Freed from impurities

_____ 18. A companion or partner

_____ 19. Bitterness

_____ 20. Person who holds opinions contrary to the beliefs of others in a group

Romeo and Juliet Vocabulary Fill In The Blanks 2 Answer Key

ORISONS	1.	Prayers
PREDOMINANT	2.	Most common or conspicuous
TRANSGRESSION	3.	Violation of a law
OBSCURED	4.	Indistinctly heard; partially hidden from the senses
PROFANERS	5.	Those showing irreverence for what is sacred
PROROGUE	6.	Discontinue a session
POSTERITY	7.	Future generations
TEDIOUS	8.	Moving or progressing very slowly
INUNDATION	9.	Covering with water; a swamping
BOISTEROUS	10.	Rough and stormy; noisy and excited
VALIDITY	11.	Good health; how sound something is
ALDERMAN	12.	A member of the municipal legislative body
PENURY	13.	Destitution
LOATHED	14.	Disliked
PRESAGE	15.	An omen
ESTEEM	16.	Regard with respect
PURGED	17.	Freed from impurities
CONSORT	18.	A companion or partner
RANCOR	19.	Bitterness
HERETIC	20.	Person who holds opinions contrary to the beliefs of others in a group

Romeo and Juliet Vocabulary Fill In The Blanks 3

_____ 1. Making something already developed greater

_____ 2. Moving or progressing very slowly

_____ 3. Foreboding

_____ 4. Destitution

_____ 5. Disliked

_____ 6. Deceived by guile

_____ 7. A member of the municipal legislative body

_____ 8. Discontinue a session

_____ 9. Be or become weak or feeble

_____ 10. Express disapproval

_____ 11. Prayers

_____ 12. Rough and stormy; noisy and excited

_____ 13. Freed from impurities

_____ 14. Causing grief

_____ 15. Those showing irreverence for what is sacred

_____ 16. A church office endowed with fixed capital assets

_____ 17. Most common or conspicuous

_____ 18. Good health; how sound something is

_____ 19. An omen

_____ 20. Regard with respect

Romeo and Juliet Vocabulary Fill In The Blanks 3 Answer Key

AUGMENTING	1. Making something already developed greater
TEDIOUS	2. Moving or progressing very slowly
PORTENTOUS	3. Foreboding
PENURY	4. Destitution
LOATHED	5. Disliked
BEGUILED	6. Deceived by guile
ALDERMAN	7. A member of the municipal legislative body
PROROGUE	8. Discontinue a session
LANGUISH	9. Be or become weak or feeble
CHIDE	10. Express disapproval
ORISONS	11. Prayers
BOISTEROUS	12. Rough and stormy; noisy and excited
PURGED	13. Freed from impurities
LAMENTABLE	14. Causing grief
PROFANERS	15. Those showing irreverence for what is sacred
BENEFICE	16. A church office endowed with fixed capital assets
PREDOMINANT	17. Most common or conspicuous
VALIDITY	18. Good health; how sound something is
PRESAGE	19. An omen
ESTEEM	20. Regard with respect

Romeo and Juliet Vocabulary Fill In The Blanks 4

_____ 1. Future generations
_____ 2. Express disapproval
_____ 3. Moving or progressing very slowly
_____ 4. Negotiating differences through an impartial third party
_____ 5. Cloak; coat
_____ 6. Evil; wicked
_____ 7. Narrate or discuss
_____ 8. Comfort in sorrow
_____ 9. Bitterness
_____ 10. A church office endowed with fixed capital assets
_____ 11. Disliked
_____ 12. Indistinctly heard; partially hidden from the senses
_____ 13. Discontinue a session
_____ 14. Causing grief
_____ 15. Person who holds opinions contrary to the beliefs of others in a group
_____ 16. Challenge the validity of something
_____ 17. Making something already developed greater
_____ 18. Violation of a law
_____ 19. Be or become weak or feeble
_____ 20. Good health; how sound something is

Romeo and Juliet Vocabulary Fill In The Blanks 4 Answer Key

POSTERITY	1. Future generations
CHIDE	2. Express disapproval
TEDIOUS	3. Moving or progressing very slowly
ARBITRATING	4. Negotiating differences through an impartial third party
MANTLE	5. Cloak; coat
PERNICIOUS	6. Evil; wicked
DISCOURSE	7. Narrate or discuss
SOLACE	8. Comfort in sorrow
RANCOR	9. Bitterness
BENEFICE	10. A church office endowed with fixed capital assets
LOATHED	11. Disliked
OBSCURED	12. Indistinctly heard; partially hidden from the senses
PROROGUE	13. Discontinue a session
LAMENTABLE	14. Causing grief
HERETIC	15. Person who holds opinions contrary to the beliefs of others in a group
IMPEACH	16. Challenge the validity of something
AUGMENTING	17. Making something already developed greater
TRANSGRESSION	18. Violation of a law
LANGUISH	19. Be or become weak or feeble
VALIDITY	20. Good health; how sound something is

Romeo and Juliet Vocabulary Matching 1

___ 1. ENVIOUS   A. Disliked
___ 2. APPERTAINING   B. Express disapproval
___ 3. ALDERMAN   C. Narrate or discuss
___ 4. ARBITRATING   D. A companion or partner
___ 5. OBSCURED   E. Causing grief
___ 6. INVOCATION   F. Violation of a law
___ 7. INUNDATION   G. Jealous
___ 8. CONSORT   H. Be or become weak or feeble
___ 9. LANGUISH   I. Indistinctly heard; partially hidden from the senses
___ 10. TEDIOUS   J. Destitution
___ 11. BEGUILED   K. Bitterness
___ 12. VALIDITY   L. Prayers
___ 13. TRANSGRESSION   M. Deceived by guile
___ 14. IMPUTE   N. Covering with water; a swamping
___ 15. LOATHED   O. Belonging to as a proper function or part
___ 16. POULTICE   P. To attribute; to credit
___ 17. PENURY   Q. A church office endowed with fixed capital assets
___ 18. ORISONS   R. A member of the municipal legislative body
___ 19. MANTLE   S. Rough and stormy; noisy and excited
___ 20. RANCOR   T. Negotiating differences through an impartial third party
___ 21. BENEFICE   U. A soft, moist mass of bread, meal or clay
___ 22. BOISTEROUS   V. Moving or progressing very slowly
___ 23. DISCOURSE   W. Cloak; coat
___ 24. LAMENTABLE   X. Incantation used in conjuring
___ 25. CHIDE   Y. Good health; how sound something is

Romeo and Juliet Vocabulary Matching 1 Answer Key

G - 1.	ENVIOUS	A. Disliked
O - 2.	APPERTAINING	B. Express disapproval
R - 3.	ALDERMAN	C. Narrate or discuss
T - 4.	ARBITRATING	D. A companion or partner
I - 5.	OBSCURED	E. Causing grief
X - 6.	INVOCATION	F. Violation of a law
N - 7.	INUNDATION	G. Jealous
D - 8.	CONSORT	H. Be or become weak or feeble
H - 9.	LANGUISH	I. Indistinctly heard; partially hidden from the senses
V - 10.	TEDIOUS	J. Destitution
M - 11.	BEGUILED	K. Bitterness
Y - 12.	VALIDITY	L. Prayers
F - 13.	TRANSGRESSION	M. Deceived by guile
P - 14.	IMPUTE	N. Covering with water; a swamping
A - 15.	LOATHED	O. Belonging to as a proper function or part
U - 16.	POULTICE	P. To attribute; to credit
J - 17.	PENURY	Q. A church office endowed with fixed capital assets
L - 18.	ORISONS	R. A member of the municipal legislative body
W - 19.	MANTLE	S. Rough and stormy; noisy and excited
K - 20.	RANCOR	T. Negotiating differences through an impartial third party
Q - 21.	BENEFICE	U. A soft, moist mass of bread, meal or clay
S - 22.	BOISTEROUS	V. Moving or progressing very slowly
C - 23.	DISCOURSE	W. Cloak; coat
E - 24.	LAMENTABLE	X. Incantation used in conjuring
B - 25.	CHIDE	Y. Good health; how sound something is

Romeo and Juliet Vocabulary Matching 2

___ 1. INUNDATION   A. Disliked
___ 2. CHIDE   B. To attribute; to credit
___ 3. LANGUISH   C. Violation of a law
___ 4. PERNICIOUS   D. Making something already developed greater
___ 5. IMPUTE   E. Foreboding
___ 6. ALDERMAN   F. Most common or conspicuous
___ 7. TEDIOUS   G. Funeral hymn or lament
___ 8. PROFANERS   H. A soft, moist mass of bread, meal or clay
___ 9. DISCOURSE   I. Rough and stormy; noisy and excited
___ 10. AUGMENTING   J. A member of the municipal legislative body
___ 11. HERETIC   K. Evil; wicked
___ 12. TRANSGRESSION   L. Narrate or discuss
___ 13. LAMENTABLE   M. Gathered; collected
___ 14. BEGUILED   N. Freed from impurities
___ 15. VALIDITY   O. Causing grief
___ 16. CULLED   P. Those showing irreverence for what is sacred
___ 17. POULTICE   Q. Covering with water; a swamping
___ 18. DIRGE   R. Person who holds opinions contrary to the beliefs of others in a group
___ 19. PORTENTOUS   S. Request earnestly
___ 20. BOISTEROUS   T. Deceived by guile
___ 21. PREDOMINANT   U. Be or become weak or feeble
___ 22. PRESAGE   V. Good health; how sound something is
___ 23. BESEECH   W. Express disapproval
___ 24. LOATHED   X. Moving or progressing very slowly
___ 25. PURGED   Y. An omen

Romeo and Juliet Vocabulary Matching 2 Answer Key

Q - 1.	INUNDATION	A.	Disliked
W - 2.	CHIDE	B.	To attribute; to credit
U - 3.	LANGUISH	C.	Violation of a law
K - 4.	PERNICIOUS	D.	Making something already developed greater
B - 5.	IMPUTE	E.	Foreboding
J - 6.	ALDERMAN	F.	Most common or conspicuous
X - 7.	TEDIOUS	G.	Funeral hymn or lament
P - 8.	PROFANERS	H.	A soft, moist mass of bread, meal or clay
L - 9.	DISCOURSE	I.	Rough and stormy; noisy and excited
D -10.	AUGMENTING	J.	A member of the municipal legislative body
R -11.	HERETIC	K.	Evil; wicked
C -12.	TRANSGRESSION	L.	Narrate or discuss
O -13.	LAMENTABLE	M.	Gathered; collected
T -14.	BEGUILED	N.	Freed from impurities
V -15.	VALIDITY	O.	Causing grief
M -16.	CULLED	P.	Those showing irreverence for what is sacred
H -17.	POULTICE	Q.	Covering with water; a swamping
G -18.	DIRGE	R.	Person who holds opinions contrary to the beliefs of others in a group
E -19.	PORTENTOUS	S.	Request earnestly
I - 20.	BOISTEROUS	T.	Deceived by guile
F -21.	PREDOMINANT	U.	Be or become weak or feeble
Y -22.	PRESAGE	V.	Good health; how sound something is
S -23.	BESEECH	W.	Express disapproval
A -24.	LOATHED	X.	Moving or progressing very slowly
N -25.	PURGED	Y.	An omen

Romeo and Juliet Vocabulary Matching 3

___ 1. OBSCURED   A. An omen
___ 2. PREDOMINANT   B. Freed from impurities
___ 3. CHIDE   C. Person who holds opinions contrary to the beliefs of others in a group
___ 4. BOISTEROUS   D. Funeral hymn or lament
___ 5. DISCOURSE   E. Discontinue a session
___ 6. ENVIOUS   F. Negotiating differences through an impartial third party
___ 7. BENEFICE   G. Jealous
___ 8. ARBITRATING   H. A member of the municipal legislative body
___ 9. ALDERMAN   I. Bitterness
___10. POULTICE   J. Narrate or discuss
___11. BESEECH   K. Evil; wicked
___12. MANTLE   L. Express disapproval
___13. ORISONS   M. Cloak; coat
___14. LAMENTABLE   N. Causing grief
___15. IMPEACH   O. Request earnestly
___16. PURGED   P. Rough and stormy; noisy and excited
___17. PROROGUE   Q. Indistinctly heard; partially hidden from the senses
___18. ESTEEM   R. Prayers
___19. PRESAGE   S. Most common or conspicuous
___20. DIRGE   T. A soft, moist mass of bread, meal or clay
___21. HERETIC   U. Regard with respect
___22. IMPUTE   V. Challenge the validity of something
___23. PERNICIOUS   W. A church office endowed with fixed capital assets
___24. BEGUILED   X. Deceived by guile
___25. RANCOR   Y. To attribute; to credit

Romeo and Juliet Vocabulary Matching 3 Answer Key

Q - 1.	OBSCURED	A. An omen
S - 2.	PREDOMINANT	B. Freed from impurities
L - 3.	CHIDE	C. Person who holds opinions contrary to the beliefs of others in a group
P - 4.	BOISTEROUS	D. Funeral hymn or lament
J - 5.	DISCOURSE	E. Discontinue a session
G - 6.	ENVIOUS	F. Negotiating differences through an impartial third party
W - 7.	BENEFICE	G. Jealous
F - 8.	ARBITRATING	H. A member of the municipal legislative body
H - 9.	ALDERMAN	I. Bitterness
T - 10.	POULTICE	J. Narrate or discuss
O - 11.	BESEECH	K. Evil; wicked
M - 12.	MANTLE	L. Express disapproval
R - 13.	ORISONS	M. Cloak; coat
N - 14.	LAMENTABLE	N. Causing grief
V - 15.	IMPEACH	O. Request earnestly
B - 16.	PURGED	P. Rough and stormy; noisy and excited
E - 17.	PROROGUE	Q. Indistinctly heard; partially hidden from the senses
U - 18.	ESTEEM	R. Prayers
A - 19.	PRESAGE	S. Most common or conspicuous
D - 20.	DIRGE	T. A soft, moist mass of bread, meal or clay
C - 21.	HERETIC	U. Regard with respect
Y - 22.	IMPUTE	V. Challenge the validity of something
K - 23.	PERNICIOUS	W. A church office endowed with fixed capital assets
X - 24.	BEGUILED	X. Deceived by guile
I - 25.	RANCOR	Y. To attribute; to credit

Romeo and Juliet Vocabulary Matching 4

___ 1. BOISTEROUS   A. A companion or partner
___ 2. IMPUTE   B. Good health; how sound something is
___ 3. PRESAGE   C. Discontinue a session
___ 4. ENMITY   D. Challenge the validity of something
___ 5. ALDERMAN   E. An omen
___ 6. TEDIOUS   F. Deep seated, often mutual hatred
___ 7. PROROGUE   G. Express disapproval
___ 8. PROFANERS   H. Incantation used in conjuring
___ 9. ENVIOUS   I. Bitterness
___10. VALIDITY   J. A member of the municipal legislative body
___11. BESEECH   K. Jealous
___12. INUNDATION   L. To attribute; to credit
___13. HERETIC   M. Cloak; coat
___14. INVOCATION   N. Funeral hymn or lament
___15. CHIDE   O. Those showing irreverence for what is sacred
___16. RANCOR   P. A soft, moist mass of bread, meal or clay
___17. PENURY   Q. Destitution
___18. CONSORT   R. Request earnestly
___19. DIRGE   S. Rough and stormy; noisy and excited
___20. IMPEACH   T. Causing grief
___21. PORTENTOUS   U. Comfort in sorrow
___22. SOLACE   V. Foreboding
___23. MANTLE   W. Covering with water; a swamping
___24. POULTICE   X. Moving or progressing very slowly
___25. LAMENTABLE   Y. Person who holds opinions contrary to the beliefs of others in a group

Romeo and Juliet Vocabulary Matching 4 Answer Key

S - 1. BOISTEROUS		A. A companion or partner
L - 2. IMPUTE		B. Good health; how sound something is
E - 3. PRESAGE		C. Discontinue a session
F - 4. ENMITY		D. Challenge the validity of something
J - 5. ALDERMAN		E. An omen
X - 6. TEDIOUS		F. Deep seated, often mutual hatred
C - 7. PROROGUE		G. Express disapproval
O - 8. PROFANERS		H. Incantation used in conjuring
K - 9. ENVIOUS		I. Bitterness
B - 10. VALIDITY		J. A member of the municipal legislative body
R - 11. BESEECH		K. Jealous
W - 12. INUNDATION		L. To attribute; to credit
Y - 13. HERETIC		M. Cloak; coat
H - 14. INVOCATION		N. Funeral hymn or lament
G - 15. CHIDE		O. Those showing irreverence for what is sacred
I - 16. RANCOR		P. A soft, moist mass of bread, meal or clay
Q - 17. PENURY		Q. Destitution
A - 18. CONSORT		R. Request earnestly
N - 19. DIRGE		S. Rough and stormy; noisy and excited
D - 20. IMPEACH		T. Causing grief
V - 21. PORTENTOUS		U. Comfort in sorrow
U - 22. SOLACE		V. Foreboding
M - 23. MANTLE		W. Covering with water; a swamping
P - 24. POULTICE		X. Moving or progressing very slowly
T - 25. LAMENTABLE		Y. Person who holds opinions contrary to the beliefs of others in a group

Romeo and Juliet Vocabulary Magic Squares 1

Match the definition with the vocabulary word. Put your answers in the magic squares below. When your answers are correct, all columns and rows will add to the same number.

A. APPERTAINING
B. DISCOURSE
C. BEGUILED
D. RANCOR
E. PROROGUE
F. ESTEEM
G. BESEECH
H. POSTERITY
I. HERETIC
J. AUGMENTING
K. ARBITRATING
L. DIRGE
M. ORISONS
N. ENVIOUS
O. POULTICE
P. PURGED

1. Belonging to as a proper function or part
2. Jealous
3. Making something already developed greater
4. Discontinue a session
5. Request earnestly
6. Funeral hymn or lament
7. Freed from impurities
8. Deceived by guile
9. A soft, moist mass of bread, meal or clay
10. Bitterness
11. Future generations
12. Negotiating differences through an impartial third party
13. Person who holds opinions contrary to the beliefs of others in a group
14. Regard with respect
15. Narrate or discuss
16. Prayers

A=	B=	C=	D=
E=	F=	G=	H=
I=	J=	K=	L=
M=	N=	O=	P=

Romeo and Juliet Vocabulary Magic Squares 1 Answer Key

Match the definition with the vocabulary word. Put your answers in the magic squares below. When your answers are correct, all columns and rows will add to the same number.

A. APPERTAINING
B. DISCOURSE
C. BEGUILED
D. RANCOR
E. PROROGUE
F. ESTEEM
G. BESEECH
H. POSTERITY
I. HERETIC
J. AUGMENTING
K. ARBITRATING
L. DIRGE
M. ORISONS
N. ENVIOUS
O. POULTICE
P. PURGED

1. Belonging to as a proper function or part
2. Jealous
3. Making something already developed greater
4. Discontinue a session
5. Request earnestly
6. Funeral hymn or lament
7. Freed from impurities
8. Deceived by guile
9. A soft, moist mass of bread, meal or clay
10. Bitterness
11. Future generations
12. Negotiating differences through an impartial third party
13. Person who holds opinions contrary to the beliefs of others in a group
14. Regard with respect
15. Narrate or discuss
16. Prayers

A=1	B=15	C=8	D=10
E=4	F=14	G=5	H=11
I=13	J=3	K=12	L=6
M=16	N=2	O=9	P=7

Romeo and Juliet Vocabulary Magic Squares 2

Match the definition with the vocabulary word. Put your answers in the magic squares below. When your answers are correct, all columns and rows will add to the same number.

A. LANGUISH
B. OBSCURED
C. ENMITY
D. POULTICE
E. CONSORT
F. INUNDATION
G. INVOCATION
H. PERNICIOUS
I. CULLED
J. CHIDE
K. ALDERMAN
L. AUGMENTING
M. BEGUILED
N. RANCOR
O. POSTERITY
P. DIRGE

1. Covering with water; a swamping
2. Gathered; collected
3. Future generations
4. A soft, moist mass of bread, meal or clay
5. Deceived by guile
6. Indistinctly heard; partially hidden from the senses
7. Evil; wicked
8. A member of the municipal legislative body
9. Deep seated, often mutual hatred
10. Funeral hymn or lament
11. Express disapproval
12. A companion or partner
13. Making something already developed greater
14. Incantation used in conjuring
15. Be or become weak or feeble
16. Bitterness

A=	B=	C=	D=
E=	F=	G=	H=
I=	J=	K=	L=
M=	N=	O=	P=

Romeo and Juliet Vocabulary Magic Squares 2 Answer Key

Match the definition with the vocabulary word. Put your answers in the magic squares below. When your answers are correct, all columns and rows will add to the same number.

A. LANGUISH
B. OBSCURED
C. ENMITY
D. POULTICE
E. CONSORT
F. INUNDATION
G. INVOCATION
H. PERNICIOUS
I. CULLED
J. CHIDE
K. ALDERMAN
L. AUGMENTING
M. BEGUILED
N. RANCOR
O. POSTERITY
P. DIRGE

1. Covering with water; a swamping
2. Gathered; collected
3. Future generations
4. A soft, moist mass of bread, meal or clay
5. Deceived by guile
6. Indistinctly heard; partially hidden from the senses
7. Evil; wicked
8. A member of the municipal legislative body
9. Deep seated, often mutual hatred
10. Funeral hymn or lament
11. Express disapproval
12. A companion or partner
13. Making something already developed greater
14. Incantation used in conjuring
15. Be or become weak or feeble
16. Bitterness

A=15	B=6	C=9	D=4
E=12	F=1	G=14	H=7
I=2	J=11	K=8	L=13
M=5	N=16	O=3	P=10

Romeo and Juliet Vocabulary Magic Squares 3

Match the definition with the vocabulary word. Put your answers in the magic squares below. When your answers are correct, all columns and rows will add to the same number.

A. VALIDITY
B. PURGED
C. PROFANERS
D. RANCOR
E. INUNDATION
F. TEDIOUS
G. CONSORT
H. BOISTEROUS
I. APPERTAINING
J. BENEFICE
K. BESEECH
L. ENVIOUS
M. LAMENTABLE
N. DISCOURSE
O. POSTERITY
P. IMPUTE

1. Those showing irreverence for what is sacred
2. A church office endowed with fixed capital assets
3. Moving or progressing very slowly
4. Future generations
5. To attribute; to credit
6. Covering with water; a swamping
7. Belonging to as a proper function or part
8. Bitterness
9. Causing grief
10. Rough and stormy; noisy and excited
11. Jealous
12. Good health; how sound something is
13. Freed from impurities
14. Request earnestly
15. A companion or partner
16. Narrate or discuss

A=	B=	C=	D=
E=	F=	G=	H=
I=	J=	K=	L=
M=	N=	O=	P=

Romeo and Juliet Vocabulary Magic Squares 3 Answer Key

Match the definition with the vocabulary word. Put your answers in the magic squares below. When your answers are correct, all columns and rows will add to the same number.

A. VALIDITY
B. PURGED
C. PROFANERS
D. RANCOR
E. INUNDATION
F. TEDIOUS
G. CONSORT
H. BOISTEROUS
I. APPERTAINING
J. BENEFICE
K. BESEECH
L. ENVIOUS
M. LAMENTABLE
N. DISCOURSE
O. POSTERITY
P. IMPUTE

1. Those showing irreverence for what is sacred
2. A church office endowed with fixed capital assets
3. Moving or progressing very slowly
4. Future generations
5. To attribute; to credit
6. Covering with water; a swamping
7. Belonging to as a proper function or part
8. Bitterness
9. Causing grief
10. Rough and stormy; noisy and excited
11. Jealous
12. Good health; how sound something is
13. Freed from impurities
14. Request earnestly
15. A companion or partner
16. Narrate or discuss

A=12	B=13	C=1	D=8
E=6	F=3	G=15	H=10
I=7	J=2	K=14	L=11
M=9	N=16	O=4	P=5

Romeo and Juliet Vocabulary Magic Squares 4

Match the definition with the vocabulary word. Put your answers in the magic squares below. When your answers are correct, all columns and rows will add to the same number.

A. PREDOMINANT
B. CONSORT
C. PURGED
D. CHIDE
E. PENURY
F. TRANSGRESSION
G. LANGUISH
H. PERNICIOUS
I. IMPEACH
J. BOISTEROUS
K. MANTLE
L. VALIDITY
M. LOATHED
N. POULTICE
O. PROFANERS
P. DISCOURSE

1. Disliked
2. Violation of a law
3. Evil; wicked
4. Those showing irreverence for what is sacred
5. Good health; how sound something is
6. Freed from impurities
7. Most common or conspicuous
8. Rough and stormy; noisy and excited
9. Cloak; coat
10. Express disapproval
11. A companion or partner
12. Challenge the validity of something
13. A soft, moist mass of bread, meal or clay
14. Destitution
15. Be or become weak or feeble
16. Narrate or discuss

A=	B=	C=	D=
E=	F=	G=	H=
I=	J=	K=	L=
M=	N=	O=	P=

Romeo and Juliet Vocabulary Magic Squares 4 Answer Key

Match the definition with the vocabulary word. Put your answers in the magic squares below. When your answers are correct, all columns and rows will add to the same number.

A. PREDOMINANT
B. CONSORT
C. PURGED
D. CHIDE
E. PENURY
F. TRANSGRESSION
G. LANGUISH
H. PERNICIOUS
I. IMPEACH
J. BOISTEROUS
K. MANTLE
L. VALIDITY
M. LOATHED
N. POULTICE
O. PROFANERS
P. DISCOURSE

1. Disliked
2. Violation of a law
3. Evil; wicked
4. Those showing irreverence for what is sacred
5. Good health; how sound something is
6. Freed from impurities
7. Most common or conspicuous
8. Rough and stormy; noisy and excited
9. Cloak; coat
10. Express disapproval
11. A companion or partner
12. Challenge the validity of something
13. A soft, moist mass of bread, meal or clay
14. Destitution
15. Be or become weak or feeble
16. Narrate or discuss

A=7	B=11	C=6	D=10
E=14	F=2	G=15	H=3
I=12	J=8	K=9	L=5
M=1	N=13	O=4	P=16

Romeo and Juliet Vocabulary Word Search 1

Words are placed backwards, forward, diagonally, up and down. Clues listed below can help you find the words. Circle the hidden vocabulary words in the maze.

```
E G A S E R P R O R O G U E S T E E M W
G N M A R B I T R A T I N G D V N S T C
C L V K Z G Y T I R E T S O P M M R B T
B U A I T R A N S G R E S S I O N U V F
Z R L M O W L Z O P N N T T C W W O G Q
B Y L L E U J D N C F N Y S M B M C T G
C E Y Z E N S L S W N I V Q I O D S H Q
R B G P S D T O J W C N C W N I X I B A
D L F U S C N A F B F U J Z V S T D P D
P K X T I J V T B S Q N N P O T K P B D
D W Y Z K L D H Z L T D D J C E E D E G
H N W F Y K E E T S E A W T A R J N N Q
O B S C U R E D P O R T E N T O U S E B
F C D P T B B V N L N I C A I U I U F Y
H K O P N E Z A H A R O I K O S M O I R
E L J N X B D L N C W N T P N B P I C K
R M A N S B B I M E I P D I R G E C E F
E A K N N O M D O N B O E S J T A I L R
T N N Y G O R I G U E U F N U P C N T Y
I Z Y C D U J T E B S L Z P U U H R N L
C D L E O Z I Y D S E T M P C R B E A K
J F R W S R X S I G E I B R R G Y P M L
P P N W K T G D H W C C A L D E R M A N
Y H B T X P M T C C H E S H D D L H Z B
```

A church office endowed with fixed capital assets (8)
A companion or partner (7)
A member of the municipal legislative body (8)
A soft, moist mass of bread, meal or clay (8)
An omen (7)
Be or become weak or feeble (8)
Belonging to as a proper function or part (12)
Bitterness (6)
Causing grief (10)
Challenge the validity of something (7)
Cloak; coat (6)
Comfort in sorrow (6)
Covering with water; a swamping (10)
Deceived by guile (8)
Deep seated, often mutual hatred (6)
Destitution (6)
Discontinue a session (8)
Disliked (7)
Evil; wicked (10)
Express disapproval (5)
Foreboding (10)

Freed from impurities (6)
Funeral hymn or lament (5)
Future generations (9)
Gathered; collected (6)
Good health; how sound something is (8)
Incantation used in conjuring (10)
Indistinctly heard; partially hidden from the senses (8)
Jealous (7)
Most common or conspicuous (11)
Moving or progressing very slowly (7)
Narrate or discuss (9)
Negotiating differences through an impartial third party (11)
Person who holds opinions contrary to the beliefs of others in a group (7)
Prayers (7)
Regard with respect (6)
Request earnestly (7)
Rough and stormy; noisy and excited (10)
To attribute; to credit (6)
Violation of a law (13)

Romeo and Juliet Vocabulary Word Search 1 Answer Key

Words are placed backwards, forward, diagonally, up and down. Clues listed below can help you find the words. Circle the hidden vocabulary words in the maze.

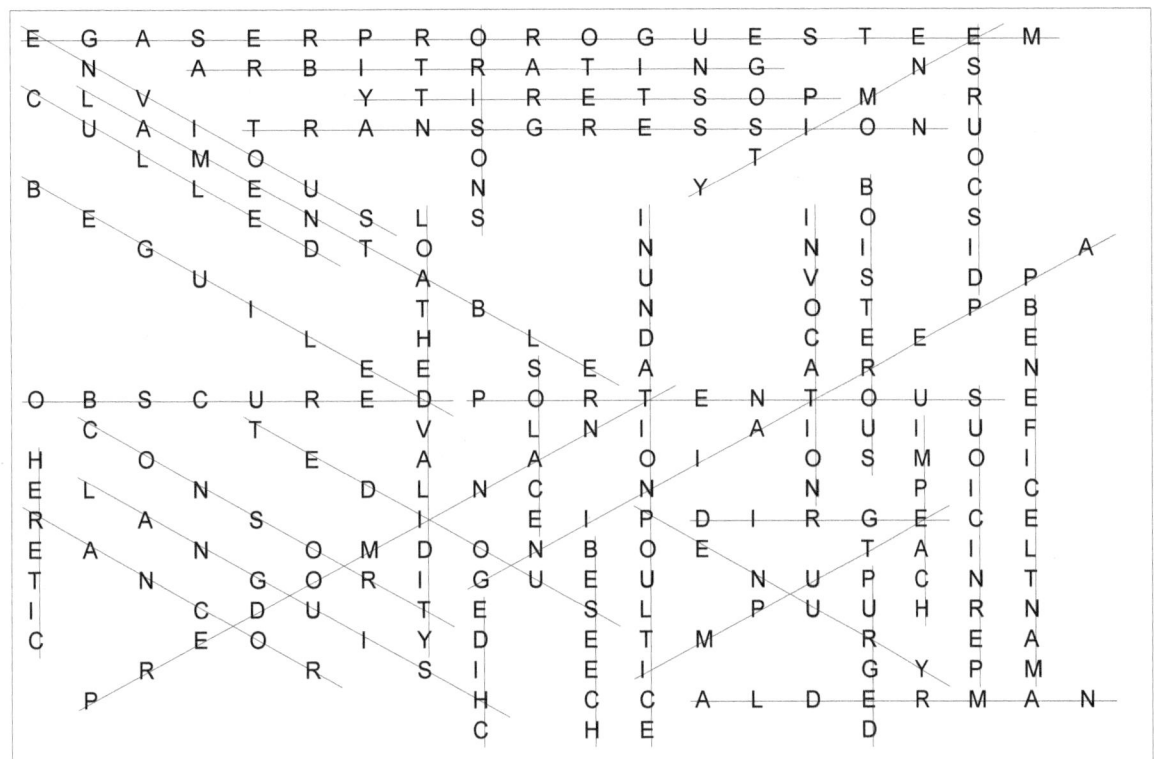

A church office endowed with fixed capital assets (8)
A companion or partner (7)
A member of the municipal legislative body (8)
A soft, moist mass of bread, meal or clay (8)
An omen (7)
Be or become weak or feeble (8)
Belonging to as a proper function or part (12)
Bitterness (6)
Causing grief (10)
Challenge the validity of something (7)
Cloak; coat (6)
Comfort in sorrow (6)
Covering with water; a swamping (10)
Deceived by guile (8)
Deep seated, often mutual hatred (6)
Destitution (6)
Discontinue a session (8)
Disliked (7)
Evil; wicked (10)
Express disapproval (5)
Foreboding (10)
Freed from impurities (6)
Funeral hymn or lament (5)
Future generations (9)
Gathered; collected (6)
Good health; how sound something is (8)
Incantation used in conjuring (10)
Indistinctly heard; partially hidden from the senses (8)
Jealous (7)
Most common or conspicuous (11)
Moving or progressing very slowly (7)
Narrate or discuss (9)
Negotiating differences through an impartial third party (11)
Person who holds opinions contrary to the beliefs of others in a group (7)
Prayers (7)
Regard with respect (6)
Request earnestly (7)
Rough and stormy; noisy and excited (10)
To attribute; to credit (6)
Violation of a law (13)

87
Copyrighted

Romeo and Juliet Vocabulary Word Search 2

Words are placed backwards, forward, diagonally, up and down. Clues listed below can help you find the words. Circle the hidden vocabulary words in the maze.

```
I M P E A C H R A N C O R C W M L O B M
T Z Q U J X V S J D O K G H N A A B K H
R Z H G V J P P J E N Z N I L N N S P G
A N S O N K R P F L S Q H D R T G C R Z
N J O R I S O N S B O A T E P L U E T
S X M O W Y F H H A R N L N M E I R D P
G P T R C X A L W T T J S D P J S E O R
R H U P Y S N M D N C R F G E P H D M S
E W Y R S F E V P E L Y N S J R N X I V
S A H E G T R S Z M W D U P Y O M T N B
S U H N N E S L O A E O Y T I M D A H
I G D V I R D V A L I D I T Y W E L N L
O M K I N Y G P L D A M A R Z G L O T S
N E P O I Z M U E B N C U P R K I A R T
P N H U A T C T J E O N E I D T U T N B
O T P S T Q Q Y T V E I D I A Q G H F D
R I R D R E S T N P J P S D Q L E E X P
T N E W E T H I K H S C N T W R B D O X
E G S V P K M R C L O U Y E E Z W U K W
N J A F P D K E V U N N K V S R L X M S
T Z G Z A R E T R I Y H D M M T O W V W
O D E B V S W S G H E R E T I C E U L Q
U J G M E K E O K C F R W C P K W E S B
S G S B S J G P E C I F E N E B K W M G
```

A church office endowed with fixed capital assets (8)
A companion or partner (7)
A member of the municipal legislative body (8)
A soft, moist mass of bread, meal or clay (8)
An omen (7)
Be or become weak or feeble (8)
Belonging to as a proper function or part (12)
Bitterness (6)
Causing grief (10)
Challenge the validity of something (7)
Cloak; coat (6)
Comfort in sorrow (6)
Covering with water; a swamping (10)
Deceived by guile (8)
Deep seated, often mutual hatred (6)
Destitution (6)
Discontinue a session (8)
Disliked (7)
Express disapproval (5)
Foreboding (10)
Freed from impurities (6)

Funeral hymn or lament (5)
Future generations (9)
Gathered; collected (6)
Good health; how sound something is (8)
Incantation used in conjuring (10)
Indistinctly heard; partially hidden from the senses (8)
Jealous (7)
Making something already developed greater (10)
Most common or conspicuous (11)
Moving or progressing very slowly (7)
Narrate or discuss (9)
Person who holds opinions contrary to the beliefs of others in a group (7)
Prayers (7)
Regard with respect (6)
Request earnestly (7)
Rough and stormy; noisy and excited (10)
Those showing irreverence for what is sacred (9)
To attribute; to credit (6)
Violation of a law (13)

Romeo and Juliet Vocabulary Word Search 2 Answer Key

Words are placed backwards, forward, diagonally, up and down. Clues listed below can help you find the words. Circle the hidden vocabulary words in the maze.

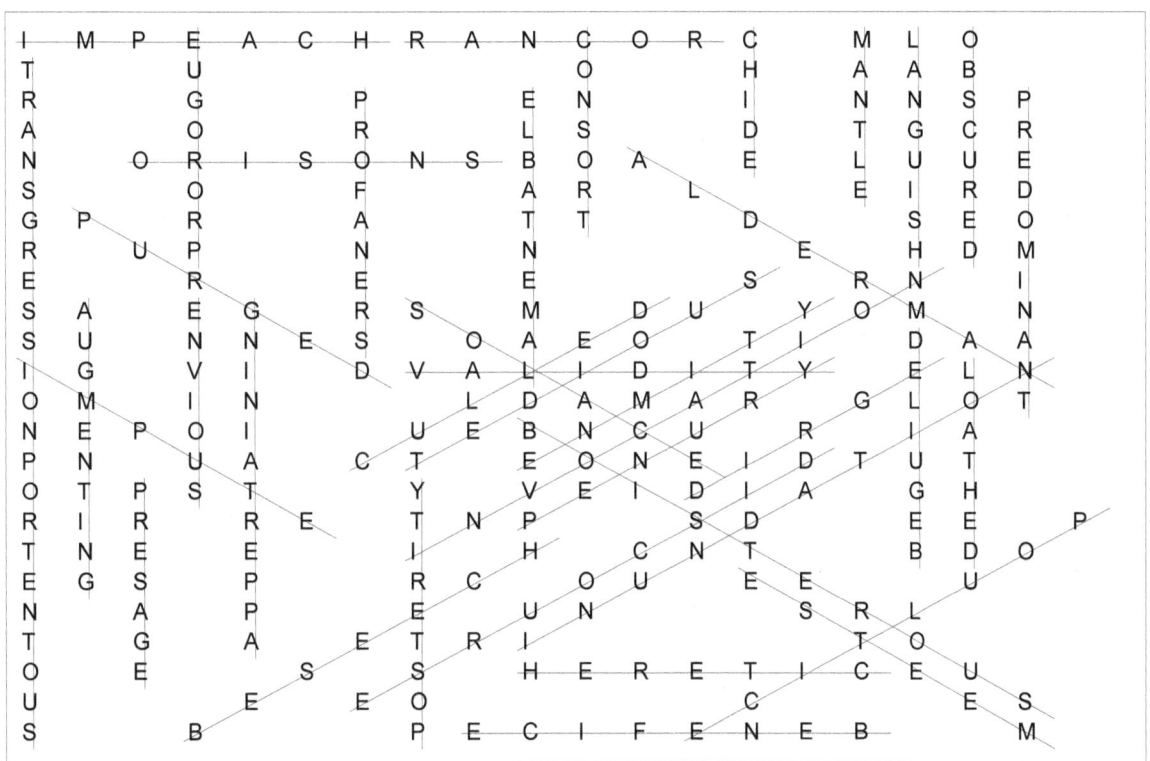

A church office endowed with fixed capital assets (8)
A companion or partner (7)
A member of the municipal legislative body (8)
A soft, moist mass of bread, meal or clay (8)
An omen (7)
Be or become weak or feeble (8)
Belonging to as a proper function or part (12)
Bitterness (6)
Causing grief (10)
Challenge the validity of something (7)
Cloak; coat (6)
Comfort in sorrow (6)
Covering with water; a swamping (10)
Deceived by guile (8)
Deep seated, often mutual hatred (6)
Destitution (6)
Discontinue a session (8)
Disliked (7)
Express disapproval (5)
Foreboding (10)
Freed from impurities (6)

Funeral hymn or lament (5)
Future generations (9)
Gathered; collected (6)
Good health; how sound something is (8)
Incantation used in conjuring (10)
Indistinctly heard; partially hidden from the senses (8)
Jealous (7)
Making something already developed greater (10)
Most common or conspicuous (11)
Moving or progressing very slowly (7)
Narrate or discuss (9)
Person who holds opinions contrary to the beliefs of others in a group (7)
Prayers (7)
Regard with respect (6)
Request earnestly (7)
Rough and stormy; noisy and excited (10)
Those showing irreverence for what is sacred (9)
To attribute; to credit (6)
Violation of a law (13)

Romeo and Juliet Vocabulary Word Search 3

Words are placed backwards, forward, diagonally, up and down. Words listed below are included in the maze. Circle the hidden vocabulary words in the maze.

```
I N V O C A T I O N K Y F C N G T B P Q
W R J M W G N I N I A T R E P P A O B K
T T G N G P R E D O M I N A N T P I T B
W M R P W M Z S C F B R Y N Y B R S C V
V J P Y W W B R S R C E J W N F O T L V
N O I T A D N U N I I T G Q V Q R E O V
L F D G N F O O Y C T S H U F D O R A C
N A L W L I X C R X E O C X I J G O T B
Y H M B D Y Z S L V R P T P M L U U H W
E S T E E M Z I M P E A C H C E E S E B
S Y T Q N R C D Z R H Y S Y D G H D B K
M C C D H T H O N Q T A L B A H Z L L Y
H T U M I Y A I N I B Z L S X C P Z P L
P P L Y S R C B D S Y H E D E N M I T Y
O R L W U I G I L D O R E M E V Y M Y F
U O E H O Z L E W E P R N B N R Q W T G
L F D U I A C K H L U P T D R S M M C M
T A S B V S O L A C E P H R O C N A R Y
I N N H N C S V S H Z U E D E S X N N D
C E O G E C H B G S Q R X N T F R T W Q
E R S T U J O I F M X G Q L U D L L Y G
S S I M D I K P D J W E X X P R N E H P
Y R R J K L S S F E X D W C M H Y Y S Q
J B O M R B W H Z B E N E F I C E S S T
```

ALDERMAN	CULLED	IMPUTE	ORISONS	PROROGUE
APPERTAINING	DIRGE	INUNDATION	PENURY	PURGED
BEGUILED	DISCOURSE	INVOCATION	PERNICIOUS	RANCOR
BENEFICE	ENMITY	LAMENTABLE	POSTERITY	SOLACE
BESEECH	ENVIOUS	LANGUISH	POULTICE	TEDIOUS
BOISTEROUS	ESTEEM	LOATHED	PREDOMINANT	VALIDITY
CHIDE	HERETIC	MANTLE	PRESAGE	
CONSORT	IMPEACH	OBSCURED	PROFANERS	

Romeo and Juliet Vocabulary Word Search 3 Answer Key

Words are placed backwards, forward, diagonally, up and down. Words listed below are included in the maze. Circle the hidden vocabulary words in the maze.

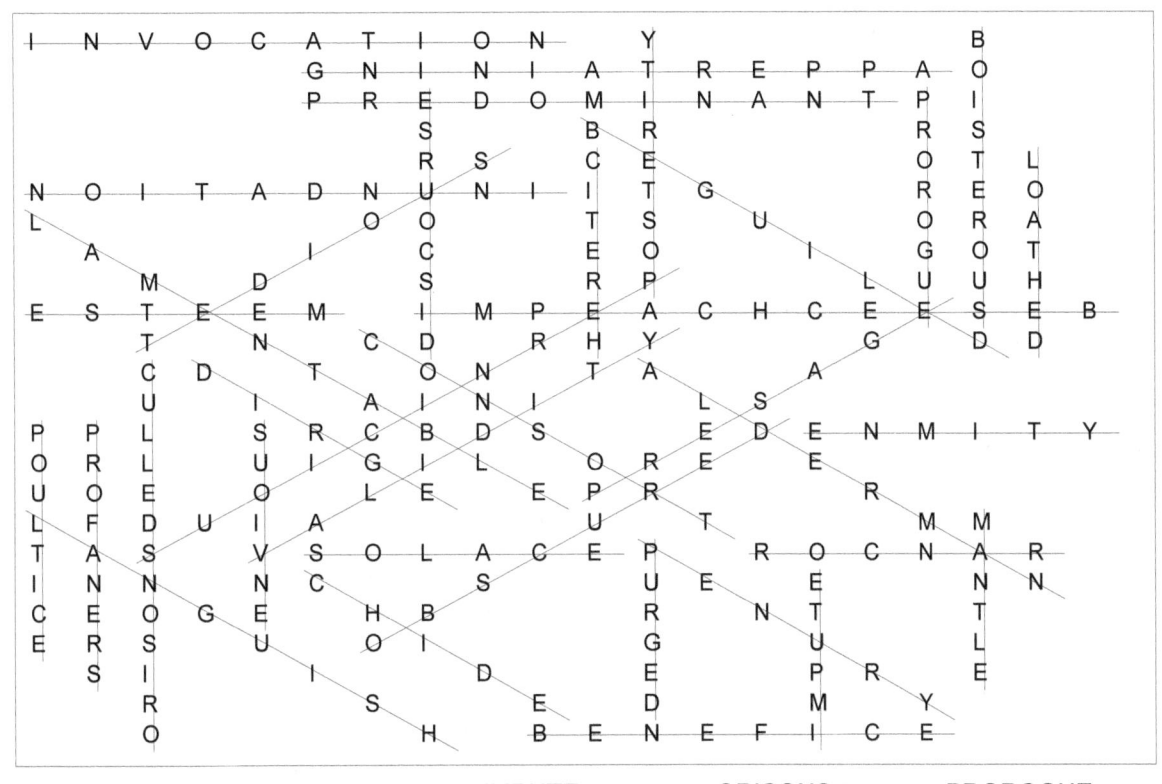

ALDERMAN	CULLED	IMPUTE	ORISONS	PROROGUE
APPERTAINING	DIRGE	INUNDATION	PENURY	PURGED
BEGUILED	DISCOURSE	INVOCATION	PERNICIOUS	RANCOR
BENEFICE	ENMITY	LAMENTABLE	POSTERITY	SOLACE
BESEECH	ENVIOUS	LANGUISH	POULTICE	TEDIOUS
BOISTEROUS	ESTEEM	LOATHED	PREDOMINANT	VALIDITY
CHIDE	HERETIC	MANTLE	PRESAGE	
CONSORT	IMPEACH	OBSCURED	PROFANERS	

Romeo and Juliet Vocabulary Word Search 4

Words are placed backwards, forward, diagonally, up and down. Words listed below are included in the maze. Circle the hidden vocabulary words in the maze.

```
P O S T E R I T Y R M K Y Z J Q C T L Y
R B O I S T E R O U S Y W G V D P K O X
O P J T R A N S G R E S S I O N U Z A Q
F R L K D N L D N W I P H T M S R V T Q
A O O J R Y E W P N X C K N Q P G F H C
N R F R F L X L U D Z S C U L E D E C
E O R G I D Z N B J U J W M Z T D A D C
R G F U B S D G P O C P Q P U K X P C Y
S U G F H A O I T G H F R P Y B Q D Y H
H E R E T I C N B N I N M E N M I T Y D
B L M I C M E V S I D I L R S S M L G H
W T O W Y T N O M N E T S E C A S D J B
N N P Z R A V C L I N M B O S R G N V Y
C W K O U R I A F A F Y U E L T V E Y Z
N P P F N B O T M T M R R M N A E M F Y
V P G B E I U I D R S E A C Q E C E D W
T A O K P T S O I E J X N L O N F E M F
E B L U B R B N R P S J C T A N R I T D
D E D I L A J S G P J S O M A U S S C Z
I S X F D T L F E A D F R N C B X O Y E
O E R Z P I I Y W H M E R S D Y L T R F
U E C R C N T C K C D D B J F B Q E W T
S C Z X X G W Y E L J O L A N G U I S H
H H Z B M W Z M A U G M E N T I N G G L
```

ALDERMAN	CULLED	INVOCATION	POULTICE
APPERTAINING	DIRGE	LAMENTABLE	PRESAGE
ARBITRATING	DISCOURSE	LANGUISH	PROFANERS
AUGMENTING	ENMITY	LOATHED	PROROGUE
BEGUILED	ENVIOUS	MANTLE	PURGED
BENEFICE	ESTEEM	OBSCURED	RANCOR
BESEECH	HERETIC	ORISONS	SOLACE
BOISTEROUS	IMPEACH	PENURY	TEDIOUS
CHIDE	IMPUTE	PORTENTOUS	TRANSGRESSION
CONSORT	INUNDATION	POSTERITY	VALIDITY

Romeo and Juliet Vocabulary Word Search 4 Answer Key

Words are placed backwards, forward, diagonally, up and down. Words listed below are included in the maze. Circle the hidden vocabulary words in the maze.

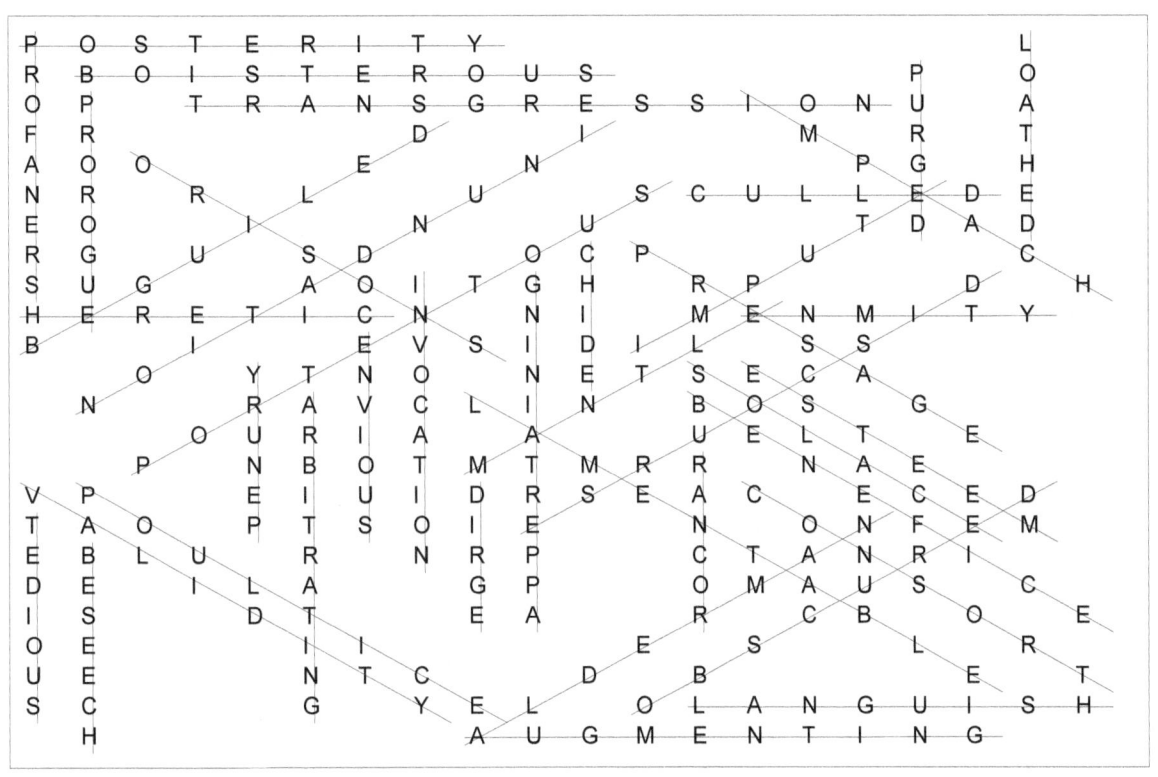

ALDERMAN	CULLED	INVOCATION	POULTICE
APPERTAINING	DIRGE	LAMENTABLE	PRESAGE
ARBITRATING	DISCOURSE	LANGUISH	PROFANERS
AUGMENTING	ENMITY	LOATHED	PROROGUE
BEGUILED	ENVIOUS	MANTLE	PURGED
BENEFICE	ESTEEM	OBSCURED	RANCOR
BESEECH	HERETIC	ORISONS	SOLACE
BOISTEROUS	IMPEACH	PENURY	TEDIOUS
CHIDE	IMPUTE	PORTENTOUS	TRANSGRESSION
CONSORT	INUNDATION	POSTERITY	VALIDITY

Romeo and Juliet Vocabulary Crossword 1

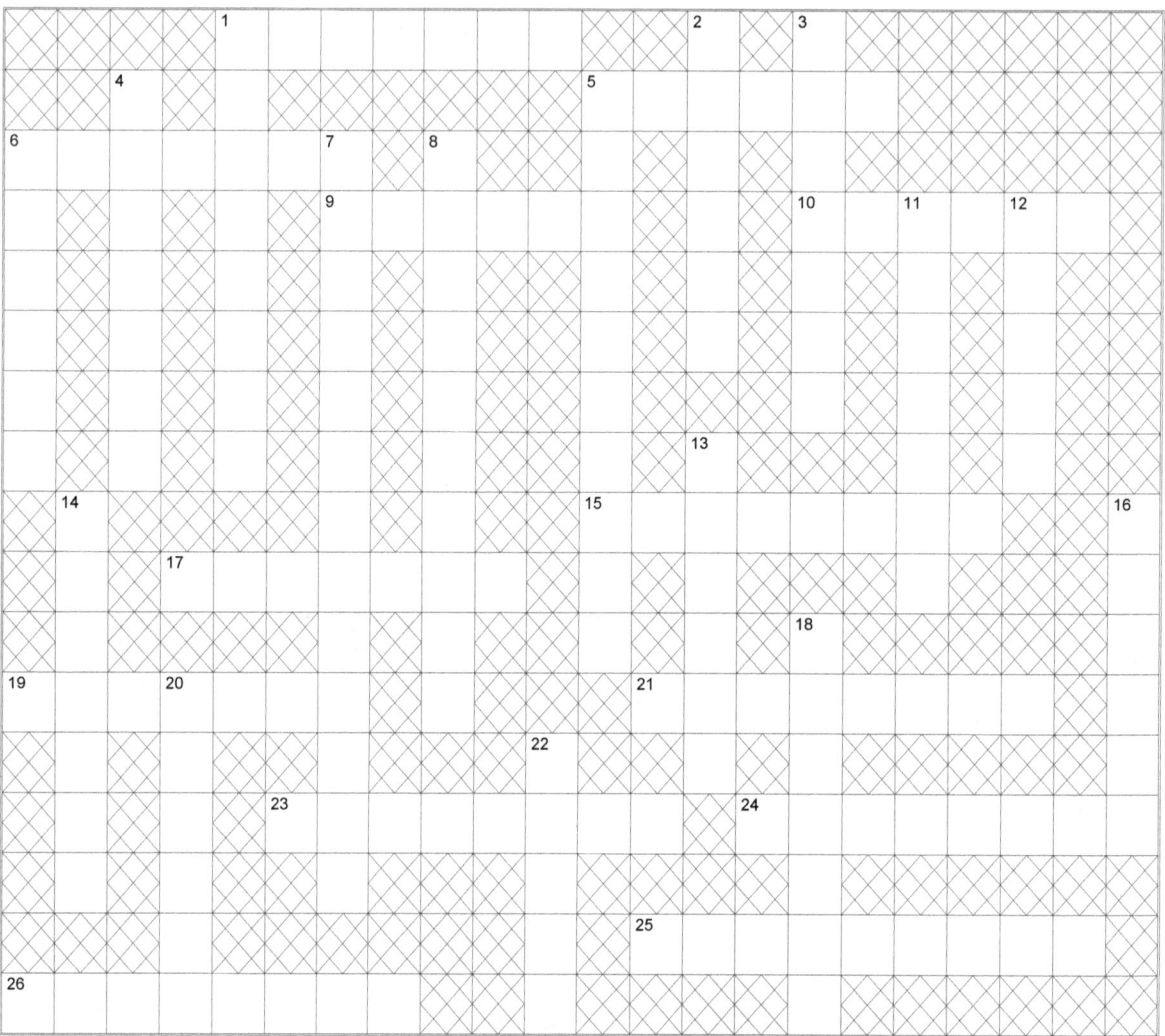

Across
1. An omen
5. Destitution
6. A companion or partner
9. Bitterness
10. Comfort in sorrow
15. Indistinctly heard; partially hidden from the senses
17. Person who holds opinions contrary to the beliefs of others in a group
19. Moving or progressing very slowly
21. A church office endowed with fixed capital assets
23. A soft, moist mass of bread, meal or clay
24. Deceived by guile
25. Narrate or discuss
26. A member of the municipal legislative body

Down
1. Discontinue a session
2. Deep seated, often mutual hatred
3. Prayers
4. Jealous
5. Foreboding
6. Gathered; collected
7. Violation of a law
8. Covering with water; a swamping
11. Disliked
12. Express disapproval
13. Regard with respect
14. Challenge the validity of something
16. Freed from impurities
18. Request earnestly
20. To attribute; to credit
22. Funeral hymn or lament

Romeo and Juliet Vocabulary Crossword 1 Answer Key

Across
1. An omen
5. Destitution
6. A companion or partner
9. Bitterness
10. Comfort in sorrow
15. Indistinctly heard; partially hidden from the senses
17. Person who holds opinions contrary to the beliefs of others in a group
19. Moving or progressing very slowly
21. A church office endowed with fixed capital assets
23. A soft, moist mass of bread, meal or clay
24. Deceived by guile
25. Narrate or discuss
26. A member of the municipal legislative body

Down
1. Discontinue a session
2. Deep seated, often mutual hatred
3. Prayers
4. Jealous
5. Foreboding
6. Gathered; collected
7. Violation of a law
8. Covering with water; a swamping
11. Disliked
12. Express disapproval
13. Regard with respect
14. Challenge the validity of something
16. Freed from impurities
18. Request earnestly
20. To attribute; to credit
22. Funeral hymn or lament

Romeo and Juliet Vocabulary Crossword 2

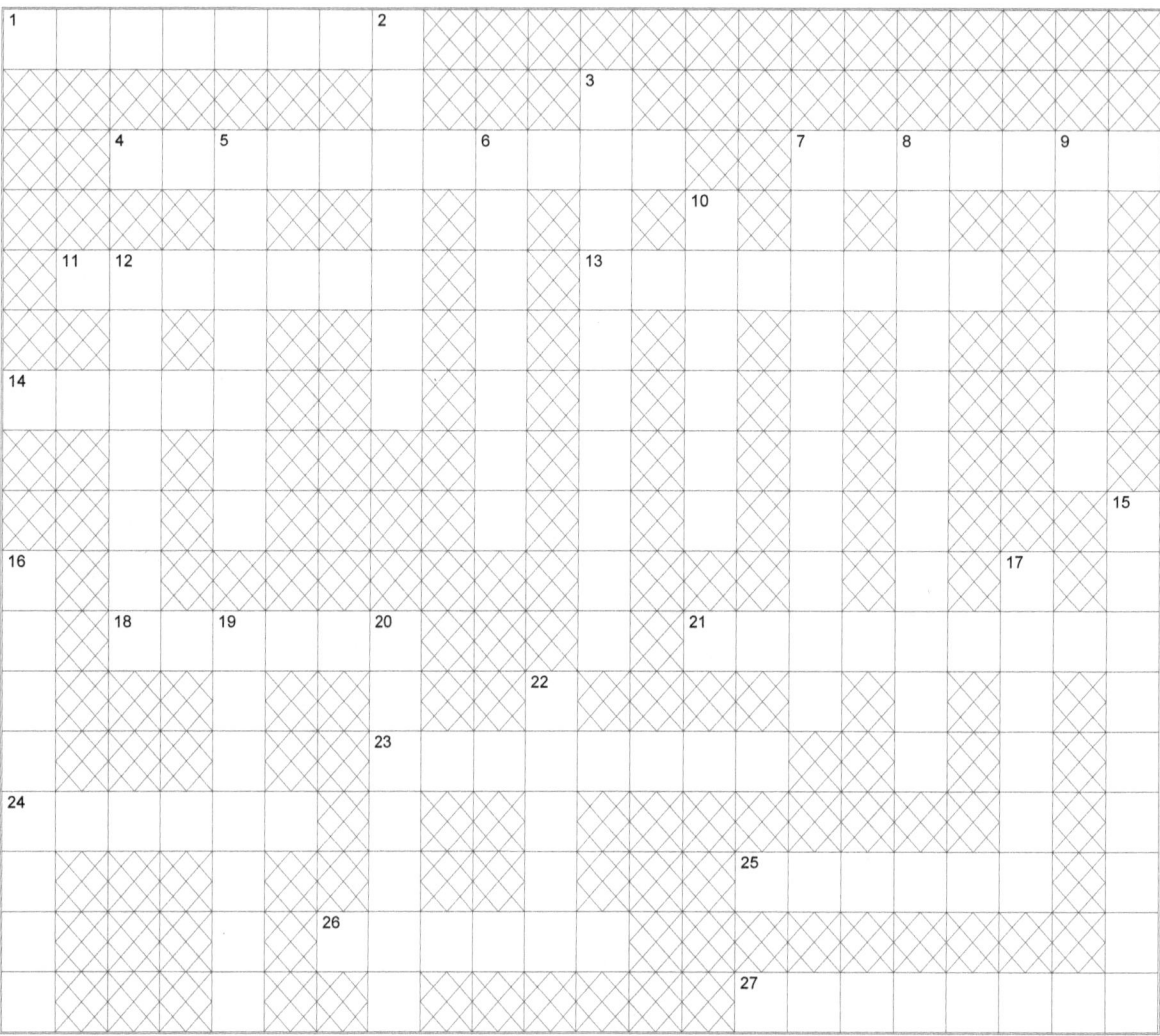

Across
1. Be or become weak or feeble
4. Negotiating differences through an impartial third party
7. Challenge the validity of something
11. A companion or partner
13. Indistinctly heard; partially hidden from the senses
14. Express disapproval
18. Comfort in sorrow
21. Those showing irreverence for what is sacred
23. Good health; how sound something is
24. To attribute; to credit
25. Deep seated, often mutual hatred
26. Freed from impurities
27. A church office endowed with fixed capital assets

Down
2. Person who holds opinions contrary to the beliefs of others in a group
3. Incantation used in conjuring
5. Request earnestly
6. Moving or progressing very slowly
7. Covering with water; a swamping
8. Most common or conspicuous
9. Gathered; collected
10. Regard with respect
12. Prayers
15. Narrate or discuss
16. Deceived by guile
17. Destitution
19. Disliked
20. Jealous
22. Funeral hymn or lament

Romeo and Juliet Vocabulary Crossword 2 Answer Key

Across
1. Be or become weak or feeble
4. Negotiating differences through an impartial third party
7. Challenge the validity of something
11. A companion or partner
13. Indistinctly heard; partially hidden from the senses
14. Express disapproval
18. Comfort in sorrow
21. Those showing irreverence for what is sacred
23. Good health; how sound something is
24. To attribute; to credit
25. Deep seated, often mutual hatred
26. Freed from impurities
27. A church office endowed with fixed capital assets

Down
2. Person who holds opinions contrary to the beliefs of others in a group
3. Incantation used in conjuring
5. Request earnestly
6. Moving or progressing very slowly
7. Covering with water; a swamping
8. Most common or conspicuous
9. Gathered; collected
10. Regard with respect
12. Prayers
15. Narrate or discuss
16. Deceived by guile
17. Destitution
19. Disliked
20. Jealous
22. Funeral hymn or lament

Romeo and Juliet Vocabulary Crossword 3

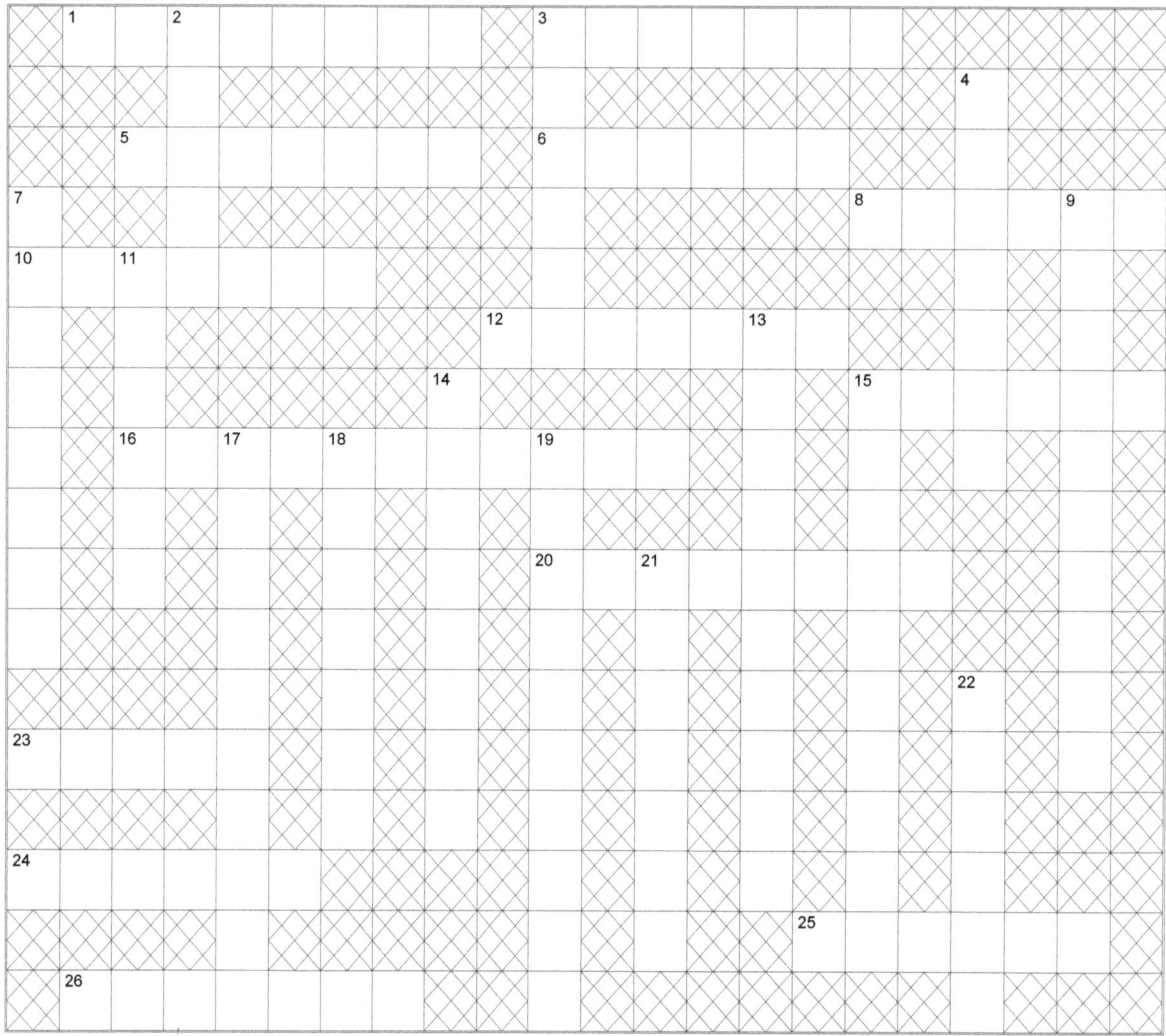

Across
1. A member of the municipal legislative body
3. Challenge the validity of something
5. Prayers
6. Destitution
8. Cloak; coat
10. Request earnestly
12. Person who holds opinions contrary to the beliefs of others in a group
15. Freed from impurities
16. Negotiating differences through an impartial third party
20. Good health; how sound something is
23. Express disapproval
24. Bitterness
25. Regard with respect
26. An omen

Down
2. Funeral hymn or lament
3. To attribute; to credit
4. A companion or partner
7. Indistinctly heard; partially hidden from the senses
9. Causing grief
11. Comfort in sorrow
13. Covering with water; a swamping
14. Be or become weak or feeble
15. Foreboding
17. Rough and stormy; noisy and excited
18. Moving or progressing very slowly
19. Incantation used in conjuring
21. Disliked
22. Gathered; collected

Romeo and Juliet Vocabulary Crossword 3 Answer Key

Across
1. A member of the municipal legislative body
3. Challenge the validity of something
5. Prayers
6. Destitution
8. Cloak; coat
10. Request earnestly
12. Person who holds opinions contrary to the beliefs of others in a group
15. Freed from impurities
16. Negotiating differences through an impartial third party
20. Good health; how sound something is
23. Express disapproval
24. Bitterness
25. Regard with respect
26. An omen

Down
2. Funeral hymn or lament
3. To attribute; to credit
4. A companion or partner
7. Indistinctly heard; partially hidden from the senses
9. Causing grief
11. Comfort in sorrow
13. Covering with water; a swamping
14. Be or become weak or feeble
15. Foreboding
17. Rough and stormy; noisy and excited
18. Moving or progressing very slowly
19. Incantation used in conjuring
21. Disliked
22. Gathered; collected

Romeo and Juliet Vocabulary Crossword 4

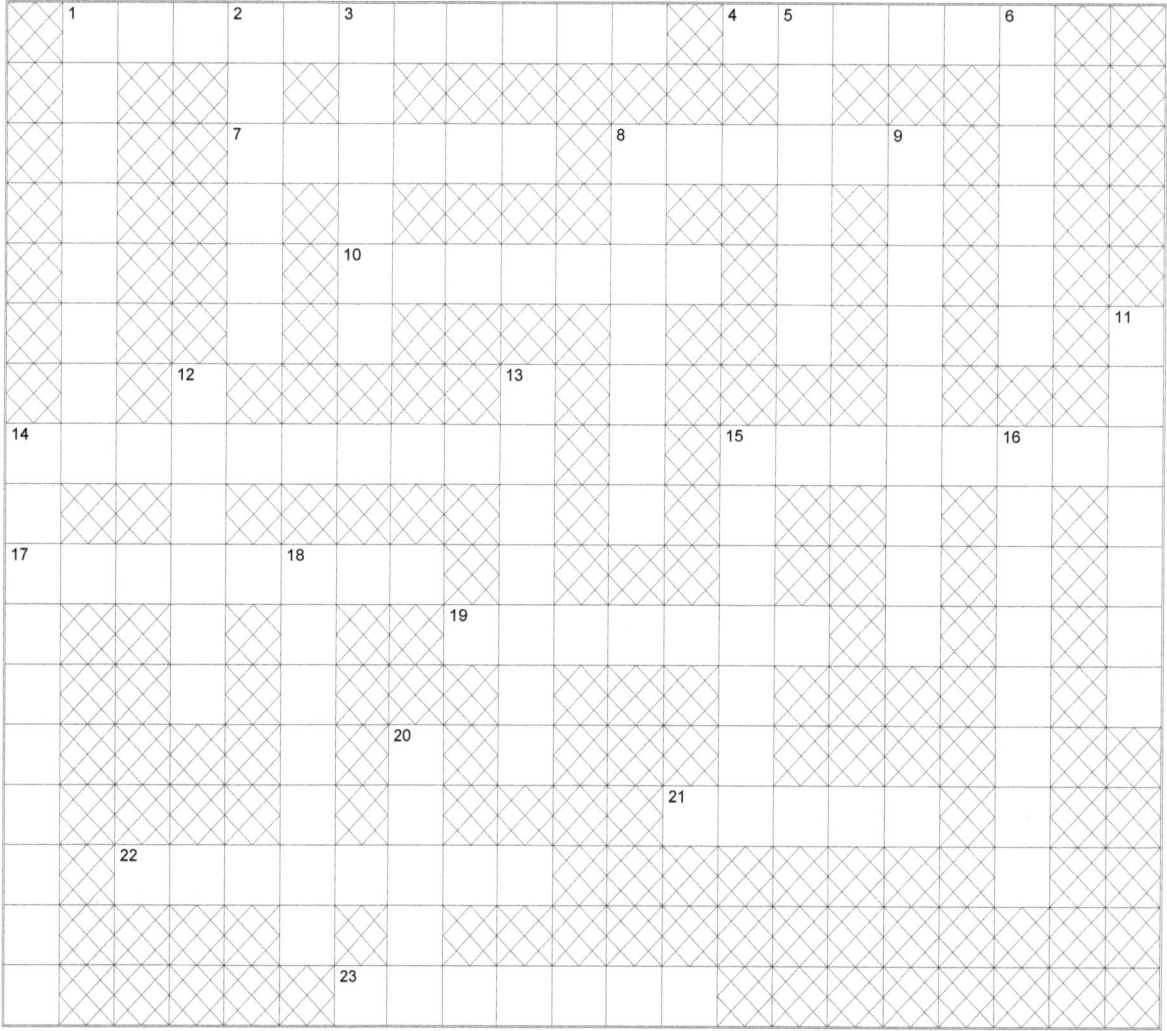

Across
1. Negotiating differences through an impartial third party
4. Regard with respect
7. Destitution
8. Gathered; collected
10. Prayers
14. Covering with water; a swamping
15. Deceived by guile
17. Good health; how sound something is
19. Disliked
21. Express disapproval
22. Indistinctly heard; partially hidden from the senses
23. Person who holds opinions contrary to the beliefs of others in a group

Down
1. A member of the municipal legislative body
2. To attribute; to credit
3. Bitterness
5. Comfort in sorrow
6. Cloak; coat
8. A companion or partner
9. Narrate or discuss
11. Moving or progressing very slowly
12. Deep seated, often mutual hatred
13. Jealous
14. Incantation used in conjuring
15. Request earnestly
16. Be or become weak or feeble
18. Challenge the validity of something
20. Funeral hymn or lament

Romeo and Juliet Vocabulary Crossword 4 Answer Key

Across
1. Negotiating differences through an impartial third party
4. Regard with respect
7. Destitution
8. Gathered; collected
10. Prayers
14. Covering with water; a swamping
15. Deceived by guile
17. Good health; how sound something is
19. Disliked
21. Express disapproval
22. Indistinctly heard; partially hidden from the senses
23. Person who holds opinions contrary to the beliefs of others in a group

Down
1. A member of the municipal legislative body
2. To attribute; to credit
3. Bitterness
5. Comfort in sorrow
6. Cloak; coat
8. A companion or partner
9. Narrate or discuss
11. Moving or progressing very slowly
12. Deep seated, often mutual hatred
13. Jealous
14. Incantation used in conjuring
15. Request earnestly
16. Be or become weak or feeble
18. Challenge the validity of something
20. Funeral hymn or lament

Romeo and Juliet Vocabulary Juggle Letters 1

1. USDOEBCR = 1. _____
   Indistinctly heard; partially hidden from the senses

2. MLRDNAAE = 2. _____
   A member of the municipal legislative body

3. HDCIE = 3. _____
   Express disapproval

4. IFNCEEEB = 4. _____
   A church office endowed with fixed capital assets

5. VOISNUE = 5. _____
   Jealous

6. RUPEGD = 6. _____
   Freed from impurities

7. HSEEEBC = 7. _____
   Request earnestly

8. RSIPUINOEC = 8. _____
   Evil; wicked

9. OHEADTL = 9. _____
   Disliked

10. YEMINT =10. _____
    Deep seated, often mutual hatred

11. MAEBLLNAET =11. _____
    Causing grief

12. GDIRE =12. _____
    Funeral hymn or lament

13. EPORNUOTST =13. _____
    Foreboding

14. UNOTADNINI =14. _____
    Covering with water; a swamping

15. EIGRRSNNASOTS =15. _____
    Violation of a law

Romeo and Juliet Vocabulary Juggle Letters 1 Answer Key

1. USDOEBCR = 1. OBSCURED
   Indistinctly heard; partially hidden from the senses

2. MLRDNAAE = 2. ALDERMAN
   A member of the municipal legislative body

3. HDCIE = 3. CHIDE
   Express disapproval

4. IFNCEEEB = 4. BENEFICE
   A church office endowed with fixed capital assets

5. VOISNUE = 5. ENVIOUS
   Jealous

6. RUPEGD = 6. PURGED
   Freed from impurities

7. HSEEEBC = 7. BESEECH
   Request earnestly

8. RSIPUINOEC = 8. PERNICIOUS
   Evil; wicked

9. OHEADTL = 9. LOATHED
   Disliked

10. YEMINT = 10. ENMITY
    Deep seated, often mutual hatred

11. MAEBLLNAET = 11. LAMENTABLE
    Causing grief

12. GDIRE = 12. DIRGE
    Funeral hymn or lament

13. EPORNUOTST = 13. PORTENTOUS
    Foreboding

14. UNOTADNINI = 14. INUNDATION
    Covering with water; a swamping

15. EIGRRSNNASOTS = 15. TRANSGRESSION
    Violation of a law

Romeo and Juliet Vocabulary Juggle Letters 2

1. TARIABIGRTN = 1. _____
Negotiating differences through an impartial third party

2. IGENTNIRAAPP = 2. _____
Belonging to as a proper function or part

3. OOITAVNICN = 3. _____
Incantation used in conjuring

4. UNGAMNEGIT = 4. _____
Making something already developed greater

5. YTNMEI = 5. _____
Deep seated, often mutual hatred

6. TOORCNS = 6. _____
A companion or partner

7. RONCAR = 7. _____
Bitterness

8. ETIPLUOC = 8. _____
A soft, moist mass of bread, meal or clay

9. ESUSDCIOR = 9. _____
Narrate or discuss

10. NLTEMA =10. _____
Cloak; coat

11. HECID =11. _____
Express disapproval

12. IGAUNLSH =12. _____
Be or become weak or feeble

13. RONFSARPE =13. _____
Those showing irreverence for what is sacred

14. IEBDEGLU =14. _____
Deceived by guile

15. DPGUER =15. _____
Freed from impurities

Romeo and Juliet Vocabulary Juggle Letters 2 Answer Key

1. TARIABIGRTN = 1. ARBITRATING
   Negotiating differences through an impartial third party

2. IGENTNIRAAPP = 2. APPERTAINING
   Belonging to as a proper function or part

3. OOITAVNICN = 3. INVOCATION
   Incantation used in conjuring

4. UNGAMNEGIT = 4. AUGMENTING
   Making something already developed greater

5. YTNMEI = 5. ENMITY
   Deep seated, often mutual hatred

6. TOORCNS = 6. CONSORT
   A companion or partner

7. RONCAR = 7. RANCOR
   Bitterness

8. ETIPLUOC = 8. POULTICE
   A soft, moist mass of bread, meal or clay

9. ESUSDCIOR = 9. DISCOURSE
   Narrate or discuss

10. NLTEMA = 10. MANTLE
    Cloak; coat

11. HECID = 11. CHIDE
    Express disapproval

12. IGAUNLSH = 12. LANGUISH
    Be or become weak or feeble

13. RONFSARPE = 13. PROFANERS
    Those showing irreverence for what is sacred

14. IEBDEGLU = 14. BEGUILED
    Deceived by guile

15. DPGUER = 15. PURGED
    Freed from impurities

Romeo and Juliet Vocabulary Juggle Letters 3

1. MSETEE = 1. _____
   Regard with respect

2. REUDPG = 2. _____
   Freed from impurities

3. ECESHEB = 3. _____
   Request earnestly

4. TIOCVONIAN = 4. _____
   Incantation used in conjuring

5. EUTIPM = 5. _____
   To attribute; to credit

6. MPACHIE = 6. _____
   Challenge the validity of something

7. CALSOE = 7. _____
   Comfort in sorrow

8. TAEMLN = 8. _____
   Cloak; coat

9. EGRNPNAIIPTA = 9. _____
   Belonging to as a proper function or part

10. ECDHI = 10. _____
    Express disapproval

11. RSGAPEE = 11. _____
    An omen

12. UPYRNE = 12. _____
    Destitution

13. RELDAMAN = 13. _____
    A member of the municipal legislative body

14. LCEDUL = 14. _____
    Gathered; collected

15. RGTAIRBTAIN = 15. _____
    Negotiating differences through an impartial third party

Romeo and Juliet Vocabulary Juggle Letters 3 Answer Key

1. MSETEE = 1. ESTEEM
Regard with respect

2. REUDPG = 2. PURGED
Freed from impurities

3. ECESHEB = 3. BESEECH
Request earnestly

4. TIOCVONIAN = 4. INVOCATION
Incantation used in conjuring

5. EUTIPM = 5. IMPUTE
To attribute; to credit

6. MPACHIE = 6. IMPEACH
Challenge the validity of something

7. CALSOE = 7. SOLACE
Comfort in sorrow

8. TAEMLN = 8. MANTLE
Cloak; coat

9. EGRNPNAIIPTA = 9. APPERTAINING
Belonging to as a proper function or part

10. ECDHI = 10. CHIDE
Express disapproval

11. RSGAPEE = 11. PRESAGE
An omen

12. UPYRNE = 12. PENURY
Destitution

13. RELDAMAN = 13. ALDERMAN
A member of the municipal legislative body

14. LCEDUL = 14. CULLED
Gathered; collected

15. RGTAIRBTAIN = 15. ARBITRATING
Negotiating differences through an impartial third party

Romeo and Juliet Vocabulary Juggle Letters 4

1. EGURRPOO = 1. _____
   Discontinue a session

2. EBINFECE = 2. _____
   A church office endowed with fixed capital assets

3. TSDEIUO = 3. _____
   Moving or progressing very slowly

4. MEIPUT = 4. _____
   To attribute; to credit

5. ETSPONUTOR = 5. _____
   Foreboding

6. NCNVOIAIOT = 6. _____
   Incantation used in conjuring

7. LEDLCU = 7. _____
   Gathered; collected

8. EHOTLDA = 8. _____
   Disliked

9. HCESEBE = 9. _____
   Request earnestly

10. LEAANMDR = 10. _____
    A member of the municipal legislative body

11. ICDEH = 11. _____
    Express disapproval

12. LEANTABMLE = 12. _____
    Causing grief

13. PTINGAINAEPR = 13. _____
    Belonging to as a proper function or part

14. CNRRAO = 14. _____
    Bitterness

15. UEOSNIV = 15. _____
    Jealous

Romeo and Juliet Vocabulary Juggle Letters 4 Answer Key

1. EGURRPOO = 1. PROROGUE
   Discontinue a session

2. EBINFECE = 2. BENEFICE
   A church office endowed with fixed capital assets

3. TSDEIUO = 3. TEDIOUS
   Moving or progressing very slowly

4. MEIPUT = 4. IMPUTE
   To attribute; to credit

5. ETSPONUTOR = 5. PORTENTOUS
   Foreboding

6. NCNVOIAIOT = 6. INVOCATION
   Incantation used in conjuring

7. LEDLCU = 7. CULLED
   Gathered; collected

8. EHOTLDA = 8. LOATHED
   Disliked

9. HCESEBE = 9. BESEECH
   Request earnestly

10. LEAANMDR =10. ALDERMAN
    A member of the municipal legislative body

11. ICDEH =11. CHIDE
    Express disapproval

12. LEANTABMLE =12. LAMENTABLE
    Causing grief

13. PTINGAINAEPR =13. APPERTAINING
    Belonging to as a proper function or part

14. CNRRAO =14. RANCOR
    Bitterness

15. UEOSNIV =15. ENVIOUS
    Jealous

ALDERMAN	A member of the municipal legislative body
APPERTAINING	Belonging to as a proper function or part
ARBITRATING	Negotiating differences through an impartial third party
AUGMENTING	Making something already developed greater
BEGUILED	Deceived by guile
BENEFICE	A church office endowed with fixed capital assets

BESEECH	Request earnestly
BOISTEROUS	Rough and stormy; noisy and excited
CHIDE	Express disapproval
CONSORT	A companion or partner
CULLED	Gathered; collected
DIRGE	Funeral hymn or lament

DISCOURSE	Narrate or discuss
ENMITY	Deep seated, often mutual hatred
ENVIOUS	Jealous
ESTEEM	Regard with respect
HERETIC	Person who holds opinions contrary to the beliefs of others in a group
IMPEACH	Challenge the validity of something

IMPUTE	To attribute; to credit
INUNDATION	Covering with water; a swamping
INVOCATION	Incantation used in conjuring
LAMENTABLE	Causing grief
LANGUISH	Be or become weak or feeble
LOATHED	Disliked

MANTLE	Cloak; coat
OBSCURED	Indistinctly heard; partially hidden from the senses
ORISONS	Prayers
PENURY	Destitution
PERNICIOUS	Evil; wicked
PORTENTOUS	Foreboding

POSTERITY	Future generations
POULTICE	A soft, moist mass of bread, meal or clay
PREDOMINANT	Most common or conspicuous
PRESAGE	An omen
PROFANERS	Those showing irreverence for what is sacred
PROROGUE	Discontinue a session

PURGED	Freed from impurities
RANCOR	Bitterness
SOLACE	Comfort in sorrow
TEDIOUS	Moving or progressing very slowly
TRANSGRESSION	Violation of a law
VALIDITY	Good health; how sound something is

Romeo and Juliet Vocabulary

BENEFICE	LANGUISH	AUGMENTING	RANCOR	IMPEACH
DISCOURSE	LAMENTABLE	DIRGE	VALIDITY	OBSCURED
ESTEEM	PORTENTOUS	FREE SPACE	POSTERITY	POULTICE
BESEECH	ORISONS	PROROGUE	APPERTAINING	BEGUILED
ARBITRATING	HERETIC	ENVIOUS	PROFANERS	SOLACE

Romeo and Juliet Vocabulary

INVOCATION	ENMITY	CULLED	PRESAGE	INUNDATION
PURGED	IMPUTE	PREDOMINANT	TRANSGRESSION	PENURY
PERNICIOUS	TEDIOUS	FREE SPACE	BOISTEROUS	CONSORT
LOATHED	CHIDE	SOLACE	PROFANERS	ENVIOUS
HERETIC	ARBITRATING	BEGUILED	APPERTAINING	PROROGUE

Romeo and Juliet Vocabulary

CONSORT	PURGED	INVOCATION	POSTERITY	VALIDITY
CULLED	BESEECH	OBSCURED	ENMITY	ESTEEM
PORTENTOUS	ORISONS	FREE SPACE	BENEFICE	PENURY
PRESAGE	ENVIOUS	ALDERMAN	HERETIC	PROROGUE
INUNDATION	BOISTEROUS	DISCOURSE	LOATHED	IMPEACH

Romeo and Juliet Vocabulary

SOLACE	LAMENTABLE	BEGUILED	TRANSGRESSION	IMPUTE
DIRGE	MANTLE	APPERTAINING	PREDOMINANT	CHIDE
POULTICE	AUGMENTING	FREE SPACE	TEDIOUS	LANGUISH
ARBITRATING	PROFANERS	IMPEACH	LOATHED	DISCOURSE
BOISTEROUS	INUNDATION	PROROGUE	HERETIC	ALDERMAN

Romeo and Juliet Vocabulary

ALDERMAN	ENVIOUS	CONSORT	IMPEACH	ESTEEM
BEGUILED	PROFANERS	CHIDE	BESEECH	PREDOMINANT
IMPUTE	AUGMENTING	FREE SPACE	LOATHED	BENEFICE
ENMITY	POULTICE	INVOCATION	PENURY	TEDIOUS
PURGED	LAMENTABLE	PRESAGE	PROROGUE	ARBITRATING

Romeo and Juliet Vocabulary

LANGUISH	DIRGE	POSTERITY	PORTENTOUS	PERNICIOUS
VALIDITY	MANTLE	INUNDATION	TRANSGRESSION	RANCOR
SOLACE	HERETIC	FREE SPACE	CULLED	DISCOURSE
ORISONS	BOISTEROUS	ARBITRATING	PROROGUE	PRESAGE
LAMENTABLE	PURGED	TEDIOUS	PENURY	INVOCATION

Romeo and Juliet Vocabulary

PENURY	HERETIC	BENEFICE	ORISONS	POSTERITY
IMPEACH	MANTLE	BOISTEROUS	LAMENTABLE	BESEECH
DISCOURSE	PRESAGE	FREE SPACE	LANGUISH	INVOCATION
VALIDITY	ESTEEM	RANCOR	PROROGUE	PREDOMINANT
INUNDATION	APPERTAINING	TEDIOUS	BEGUILED	IMPUTE

Romeo and Juliet Vocabulary

PERNICIOUS	PORTENTOUS	AUGMENTING	CULLED	TRANSGRESSION
ENVIOUS	OBSCURED	PROFANERS	ENMITY	PURGED
ALDERMAN	ARBITRATING	FREE SPACE	DIRGE	POULTICE
CHIDE	CONSORT	IMPUTE	BEGUILED	TEDIOUS
APPERTAINING	INUNDATION	PREDOMINANT	PROROGUE	RANCOR

Romeo and Juliet Vocabulary

POSTERITY	ORISONS	VALIDITY	DIRGE	PENURY
MANTLE	INVOCATION	PERNICIOUS	PRESAGE	BEGUILED
PROROGUE	PURGED	FREE SPACE	ENVIOUS	DISCOURSE
IMPEACH	BESEECH	SOLACE	HERETIC	POULTICE
TEDIOUS	LANGUISH	CHIDE	PORTENTOUS	CONSORT

Romeo and Juliet Vocabulary

BENEFICE	AUGMENTING	ARBITRATING	LAMENTABLE	IMPUTE
RANCOR	PROFANERS	ENMITY	LOATHED	ESTEEM
OBSCURED	TRANSGRESSION	FREE SPACE	INUNDATION	ALDERMAN
PREDOMINANT	BOISTEROUS	CONSORT	PORTENTOUS	CHIDE
LANGUISH	TEDIOUS	POULTICE	HERETIC	SOLACE

Romeo and Juliet Vocabulary

LANGUISH	INUNDATION	VALIDITY	IMPUTE	LAMENTABLE
MANTLE	BEGUILED	BENEFICE	APPERTAINING	POULTICE
ORISONS	CONSORT	FREE SPACE	CHIDE	IMPEACH
PROFANERS	OBSCURED	AUGMENTING	ENMITY	DISCOURSE
PRESAGE	BESEECH	ALDERMAN	PERNICIOUS	PORTENTOUS

Romeo and Juliet Vocabulary

PROROGUE	ENVIOUS	PURGED	HERETIC	ARBITRATING
PREDOMINANT	TRANSGRESSION	RANCOR	LOATHED	TEDIOUS
ESTEEM	POSTERITY	FREE SPACE	BOISTEROUS	CULLED
DIRGE	SOLACE	PORTENTOUS	PERNICIOUS	ALDERMAN
BESEECH	PRESAGE	DISCOURSE	ENMITY	AUGMENTING

Romeo and Juliet Vocabulary

APPERTAINING	LAMENTABLE	ALDERMAN	PRESAGE	ARBITRATING
MANTLE	IMPEACH	LOATHED	DISCOURSE	ORISONS
INUNDATION	AUGMENTING	FREE SPACE	INVOCATION	LANGUISH
RANCOR	PORTENTOUS	PROROGUE	DIRGE	TEDIOUS
IMPUTE	VALIDITY	PURGED	ENVIOUS	POSTERITY

Romeo and Juliet Vocabulary

POULTICE	HERETIC	OBSCURED	CONSORT	BESEECH
SOLACE	CULLED	PERNICIOUS	BENEFICE	CHIDE
PROFANERS	PREDOMINANT	FREE SPACE	TRANSGRESSION	ESTEEM
PENURY	BOISTEROUS	POSTERITY	ENVIOUS	PURGED
VALIDITY	IMPUTE	TEDIOUS	DIRGE	PROROGUE

Romeo and Juliet Vocabulary

PENURY	SOLACE	LAMENTABLE	ORISONS	INVOCATION
ALDERMAN	BOISTEROUS	CONSORT	POULTICE	ESTEEM
CULLED	OBSCURED	FREE SPACE	BESEECH	AUGMENTING
LOATHED	PREDOMINANT	BENEFICE	ARBITRATING	PERNICIOUS
BEGUILED	IMPUTE	PORTENTOUS	PROFANERS	PURGED

Romeo and Juliet Vocabulary

MANTLE	RANCOR	APPERTAINING	ENMITY	IMPEACH
HERETIC	DISCOURSE	DIRGE	VALIDITY	TEDIOUS
CHIDE	LANGUISH	FREE SPACE	TRANSGRESSION	POSTERITY
PROROGUE	ENVIOUS	PURGED	PROFANERS	PORTENTOUS
IMPUTE	BEGUILED	PERNICIOUS	ARBITRATING	BENEFICE

Romeo and Juliet Vocabulary

POSTERITY	INVOCATION	BEGUILED	VALIDITY	OBSCURED
PURGED	HERETIC	CULLED	PERNICIOUS	DISCOURSE
INUNDATION	CHIDE	FREE SPACE	ALDERMAN	BENEFICE
ESTEEM	BESEECH	LOATHED	PENURY	ARBITRATING
DIRGE	IMPUTE	TEDIOUS	TRANSGRESSION	ENMITY

Romeo and Juliet Vocabulary

AUGMENTING	LANGUISH	PRESAGE	ENVIOUS	PROFANERS
PREDOMINANT	RANCOR	PORTENTOUS	LAMENTABLE	BOISTEROUS
MANTLE	SOLACE	FREE SPACE	PROROGUE	POULTICE
ORISONS	CONSORT	ENMITY	TRANSGRESSION	TEDIOUS
IMPUTE	DIRGE	ARBITRATING	PENURY	LOATHED

Romeo and Juliet Vocabulary

AUGMENTING	PORTENTOUS	PREDOMINANT	PROROGUE	PURGED
RANCOR	POULTICE	ALDERMAN	DISCOURSE	LANGUISH
POSTERITY	PROFANERS	FREE SPACE	HERETIC	BEGUILED
CONSORT	IMPUTE	ORISONS	CHIDE	VALIDITY
TRANSGRESSION	ENMITY	PENURY	LAMENTABLE	OBSCURED

Romeo and Juliet Vocabulary

APPERTAINING	TEDIOUS	DIRGE	LOATHED	BENEFICE
ENVIOUS	ESTEEM	CULLED	ARBITRATING	PERNICIOUS
IMPEACH	INVOCATION	FREE SPACE	BESEECH	SOLACE
MANTLE	PRESAGE	OBSCURED	LAMENTABLE	PENURY
ENMITY	TRANSGRESSION	VALIDITY	CHIDE	ORISONS

Romeo and Juliet Vocabulary

PURGED	HERETIC	CHIDE	IMPEACH	CONSORT
ALDERMAN	INUNDATION	PORTENTOUS	SOLACE	ENMITY
PERNICIOUS	BENEFICE	FREE SPACE	ARBITRATING	APPERTAINING
INVOCATION	PROFANERS	AUGMENTING	ENVIOUS	OBSCURED
DIRGE	PENURY	TEDIOUS	RANCOR	PROROGUE

Romeo and Juliet Vocabulary

DISCOURSE	POSTERITY	PREDOMINANT	LANGUISH	POULTICE
TRANSGRESSION	IMPUTE	CULLED	ORISONS	LOATHED
VALIDITY	ESTEEM	FREE SPACE	BOISTEROUS	BEGUILED
MANTLE	BESEECH	PROROGUE	RANCOR	TEDIOUS
PENURY	DIRGE	OBSCURED	ENVIOUS	AUGMENTING

Romeo and Juliet Vocabulary

ORISONS	INUNDATION	PURGED	BOISTEROUS	ALDERMAN
PROROGUE	IMPEACH	TRANSGRESSION	CONSORT	HERETIC
LOATHED	CHIDE	FREE SPACE	CULLED	ESTEEM
BEGUILED	ARBITRATING	ENMITY	SOLACE	PERNICIOUS
PRESAGE	RANCOR	INVOCATION	LANGUISH	POULTICE

Romeo and Juliet Vocabulary

AUGMENTING	IMPUTE	VALIDITY	PROFANERS	APPERTAINING
ENVIOUS	DIRGE	LAMENTABLE	DISCOURSE	MANTLE
PORTENTOUS	BENEFICE	FREE SPACE	PENURY	TEDIOUS
PREDOMINANT	OBSCURED	POULTICE	LANGUISH	INVOCATION
RANCOR	PRESAGE	PERNICIOUS	SOLACE	ENMITY

Romeo and Juliet Vocabulary

BOISTEROUS	PURGED	ARBITRATING	PERNICIOUS	LAMENTABLE
DIRGE	ESTEEM	IMPUTE	PROROGUE	LANGUISH
OBSCURED	PRESAGE	FREE SPACE	BENEFICE	IMPEACH
ENVIOUS	PROFANERS	CULLED	INVOCATION	APPERTAINING
CHIDE	ENMITY	AUGMENTING	POSTERITY	BEGUILED

Romeo and Juliet Vocabulary

RANCOR	PORTENTOUS	HERETIC	MANTLE	TRANSGRESSION
LOATHED	PREDOMINANT	SOLACE	ORISONS	DISCOURSE
INUNDATION	CONSORT	FREE SPACE	POULTICE	BESEECH
ALDERMAN	TEDIOUS	BEGUILED	POSTERITY	AUGMENTING
ENMITY	CHIDE	APPERTAINING	INVOCATION	CULLED

Romeo and Juliet Vocabulary

PRESAGE	INVOCATION	RANCOR	LAMENTABLE	IMPUTE
IMPEACH	PROFANERS	PURGED	BEGUILED	ESTEEM
PERNICIOUS	HERETIC	FREE SPACE	PREDOMINANT	AUGMENTING
LOATHED	APPERTAINING	CONSORT	OBSCURED	PORTENTOUS
BESEECH	INUNDATION	ARBITRATING	POSTERITY	ENVIOUS

Romeo and Juliet Vocabulary

CHIDE	DISCOURSE	DIRGE	BOISTEROUS	ORISONS
TEDIOUS	ALDERMAN	BENEFICE	POULTICE	TRANSGRESSION
ENMITY	VALIDITY	FREE SPACE	PENURY	MANTLE
CULLED	LANGUISH	ENVIOUS	POSTERITY	ARBITRATING
INUNDATION	BESEECH	PORTENTOUS	OBSCURED	CONSORT

Romeo and Juliet Vocabulary

OBSCURED	APPERTAINING	POSTERITY	CHIDE	ENVIOUS
TEDIOUS	ORISONS	PURGED	ARBITRATING	MANTLE
RANCOR	LOATHED	FREE SPACE	LAMENTABLE	BEGUILED
INUNDATION	DISCOURSE	CULLED	CONSORT	VALIDITY
PRESAGE	BOISTEROUS	ENMITY	PORTENTOUS	IMPUTE

Romeo and Juliet Vocabulary

TRANSGRESSION	BESEECH	BENEFICE	PROFANERS	ALDERMAN
IMPEACH	AUGMENTING	LANGUISH	POULTICE	INVOCATION
PREDOMINANT	HERETIC	FREE SPACE	PERNICIOUS	SOLACE
PROROGUE	DIRGE	IMPUTE	PORTENTOUS	ENMITY
BOISTEROUS	PRESAGE	VALIDITY	CONSORT	CULLED

Romeo and Juliet Vocabulary

BESEECH	SOLACE	CHIDE	ENVIOUS	TRANSGRESSION
CULLED	DISCOURSE	CONSORT	ENMITY	LOATHED
LAMENTABLE	IMPUTE	FREE SPACE	POULTICE	LANGUISH
APPERTAINING	ESTEEM	ALDERMAN	PROROGUE	AUGMENTING
PORTENTOUS	PROFANERS	ORISONS	POSTERITY	INUNDATION

Romeo and Juliet Vocabulary

BEGUILED	ARBITRATING	PERNICIOUS	PENURY	BENEFICE
VALIDITY	DIRGE	PRESAGE	PURGED	RANCOR
PREDOMINANT	HERETIC	FREE SPACE	TEDIOUS	INVOCATION
BOISTEROUS	MANTLE	INUNDATION	POSTERITY	ORISONS
PROFANERS	PORTENTOUS	AUGMENTING	PROROGUE	ALDERMAN

www.ingramcontent.com/pod-product-compliance
Lightning Source LLC
LaVergne TN
LVHW081538060526
838200LV00048B/2128